Amish C
The Complete Series

By Sarah Price
New and Expanded for 2014
With Recipes, Hymns,
and an Excerpt from
Sarah Price's Best Selling
Plain Fame Trilogy

Price Publishing LLC.
2014

The Pennsylvania Dutch used in this manuscript is taken from the Pennsylvania Dutch Revised Dictionary (1991) by C. Richard Beam, Brookshire Publications, Inc. in Lancaster, PA.

Other Books by Sarah Price

The Amish of Lancaster Series

#1: Fields of Corn

#2: Hills of Wheat

#3: Pastures of Faith
#4: Valley of Hope

The Amish of Ephrata Series

#1: The Tomato Patch

#2: The Quilting Bee

#3: The Hope Chest
#4: The Clothes Line

The Plain Fame Trilogy

Plain Fame
Plain Change
Plain Again

Other Amish Christian Romances

Amish Circle Letters
Amish Circle Letters II

A Gift of Faith: An Amish Christmas Story

An Amish Christmas Carol: Amish Christian Classic Series

A Christmas Gift for Rebecca: An Amish Christian Romance
Gettysburg's Chosen Sons

The Adventures of a Family Dog Series

#1: A Small Dog Named Peek-a-boo

#2: Peek-a-boo Runs Away

#3: Peek-a-boo's New Friends
#4: Peek-a-boo and Daisy Doodle (2013)

Other Books, Novellas and Short Stories

Gypsy in Black
Postcards from Abby (with Ella Stewart)
Meet Me in Heaven (with Ella Stewart)
The Prayer Chain Series (with Ella Stewart)

Table of Contents

Foreword

Writing about the wonderful culture and religion of the Amish people is something that I have been doing for over twenty-five years. As many of my readers may have noticed, my novels, novellas and short stories present an authentic glimpse into the lives of the Amish, a glimpse that comes from my growing up Mennonite and having lived among the Amish since I was nineteen years old.

Most of my stories are love stories. Whether you are reading about Shana and Emanuel's struggle to balance the differences of their upbringing with their love for each other (Fields of Corn) or Amanda and Alejandro trying to find a way to survive the clash of their individual and very different cultures (The Plain Fame Trilogy), there is a degree of love written in the stories.

This book and its sequel, Amish Circle Letters II, are a bit unusual. Many of us admire the Amish, viewing their culture and religion as idyllic, a step back in time to a place where stress and technology are foreign words.

That image is actually quite far from the truth.

The Amish are people, just like you and I. They, too, struggle with relationships, disappointments, questions of faith, and even temptations, a fact that some Christians might not want to know, but nevertheless, does exist among the Plain people as well.

When I first heard the term "circle letters", I was immediately enthralled. As a woman of the 21st century, I grew up with technology and social media, both of which have become engrained in my life. It's how I communicate with my children, my family, my friends, and my readers.

Unlike the Englischers, Amish do not use technology. Typically, several families will share a telephone that is always located outside of the home. A message left on a communal voice message system might take a few days to be retrieved and even longer to be returned.

So how do the Amish communicate?

Letters.

Often, groups of Amish will write letters and send them with a list of addresses of people that they would like to include in the correspondence. Since they do not have access to photocopiers, the first person on the list will receive the letter, read it, and respond. That person sends both the first letter and their response to the second name on the list. This continues until the entire package of letters goes full-circle, returning to the original sender.

At this point, the original begins a second circle and start the process of over again. It's a wonderful way to stay in touch and something that the families look forward to receiving.

This series of books follows one family, Miriam Fisher and her seven children. You will read their letters as they travel throughout the circle. I hope you enjoy the series as much as I have enjoyed researching and writing it.

Finally, you should know that all of the stories that you are going to read are based on true stories, stories that happened within the very Amish community where I share a home with an Amish woman. However, names and locations have been changed and I have taken the liberty of greatly embellishing them, something all good stories need.

Blessings,

Sarah Price

http://www.sarahpriceauthor.com

http://www.facebook.com/fansofsarahprice

Twitter: @SarahPriceAmish

A Note About Vocabulary

The Amish speak Pennsylvania Dutch (also called Amish German or Amish Dutch). This is a verbal language with variations in spelling among communities throughout the USA. For example, in some regions, a grandfather is "*grossdaadi*" while in other regions he is known as "*grossdawdi*".

In addition, there are words such a "mayhaps" or the use of the word "then" at the end of sentences and, my favorite, "for sure and certain" which are not necessarily from the Pennsylvania Dutch language/dialect, but are unique to the Amish.

The use of these words comes from my own experience living among the Amish in Lancaster County, Pennsylvania.

For your convenience, a glossary of terms is provided at the end of the book.

Chapter One: Miriam's Letter

Dear Children,

It seems that a quiet has fallen upon our lives. Daed and I are finally settling into the grossdaadihaus with brother Steve, John David, and sister Mary Ruth. While smaller, it is just as cozy as the main house, which suits Isaac and his growing family nicely.

Your daed, Steve, and John David are keeping busy helping Isaac with the farm, although Steve is still working his own farm across the lane. I'm sure he'd like to move in there one day, but being alone, the farm is better tended by his tenants.

Your sister Mary Ruth has been helping John and sister Sylvia with their new market-stand in Maryland on Thursdays and Fridays. Those are long days for your sister but she seems to enjoy it. She comes home with the most unbelievable stories about the crazy things those Englischers say to her.

Isaac's Anna is keeping me busy. I've been helping with her kinner while she's working the dairy with Isaac. It's a blessing to have the young children living in our old house, that's for sure and certain...although I sure do find myself making more cookies than I remember in days past. Anna's young Katie keeps us all busy with her questions.

Speaking of Englischers, we had a visit from Eleanor Haile again. She has been stopping by more regular-like... about once a month, I reckon. I missed seeing her, being that I was at my sister's. But she visited with Anna last week for a while. She even brought the kinner some whoopie pies. Benjamin and Katie made certain to tell me all about their sweet treat.

Let us not let time and distance keep us apart. I have wanted to send this letter to all of you, to ask that you contribute your own letter to the package and send it along to the next family on the list. In that way, as we pass along the circle letters, we can all stay connected, despite the fact that we all lead such very busy lives and barely ever see each other.

I look forward to receiving all of your letters when the circle returns to me. In the meantime, I will pray for each and every one of you. May God keep and protect you and your families.

Love,

Mother

Miriam sat down at the old wooden farmers' table in her kitchen and stared at the piece of paper before her. She had waited a long time to write this letter. In fact, she had spent a long time praying about whether or not she should write this letter. She knew that her children were busy with their own families and didn't have much time for correspondence, especially in the summer months. However, with all of her children grown and most of them living in different towns, she missed knowing what was happening in their lives. She missed the casual conversations at suppertime. She missed being an intricate part of their lives.

Certainly, a circle letter would help them to stay connected. It was, indeed, a right *gut* idea. Or so she felt after weeks of praying about it.

She glanced over the list of names and addresses jotted down on the sheet of paper. They were all there…her six children that no longer lived at home. Most had settled in nearby towns on farms of their own, although several were living in more contemporary houses and working at market stands or local shops. There just wasn't enough land to go around to satisfy every young couple that desired to have their own farm. Many of these farms were now under sixty acres, not enough to sustain a large Amish family, never mind two or three families that often resided on the property.

There were three others siblings still living at home. Mary Ruth was the youngest child, a serious, yet sometimes, petulant, twenty-one year old. With brown hair and chocolate brown eyes, she was a pretty girl but there was little sign of any courtship going on. Miriam was concerned about her. The older women got, the harder it was to marry. At twenty-one, she should have been married by now.

Her twenty-three year old son, John David was a different story. He was clearly paving the path for marriage this fall. His intended was a delightful young woman, Ella Riehl from Paradise. It was a few towns over and Miriam never could quite figure out how they had met up but she was certain that Ella was a fine young woman. Her family was most reputable as being godly and good, full of kindness and compassion for everyone and very helpful within the community. Miriam was most pleased with that match and prayed that, indeed, there would be an autumn wedding.

And then there was Steve. At thirty-four years old, he was a *leddich,* a bachelor with little to no chance of getting married anytime soon…if at all. He was too old to hang out with the youth groups and rarely socialized with his friends, all of whom were long married and had several children of their own. Miriam worried about Steve, suspecting that he'd remain unmarried with no one to take care of him as he aged. Although he kept repeating that him not being married was obviously what God had in his plan for him, that fact weighted heavily on Miriam's heart.

Yet, despite being older and single, Steve had acquired a large farm directly across the lane from their own. That certainly confused her. With no intentions of marrying, he certainly didn't need such a big farm. Of course, he didn't live there. Instead, he rented the main house to another Amish family and helped them with the cows. A godly man and a very hard worker indeed, Miriam thought with just a little bit of pride, she admitted.

"You finished your letter yet, then?"

Miriam looked up, surprised to see her youngest daughter, Mary Ruth, walk into the kitchen. As always, she was barefoot and wore an old, blue bandana over her head instead of her prayer *kapp*. It was a bone of contention with Miriam that her daughter refused to wear her prayer *kapp* at home unless it was for a formal occasion. "You home already, I see."

"Ja," Mary Ruth said as she walked over to the kitchen sink to wash her hands, ignoring her mamm's look of disapproval. "Helped Anna making cheese. It's pressing now." Wiping her hands on the fresh kitchen towel, she turned around and smiled at her mother. "Little Katie was there helping too."

"No doubt!" Miriam smiled, slowly forgetting her frustration with Mary Ruth. The mention of her granddaughter, Katie, always brought a smile to her face.

"She's something else," Mary Ruth offered. "I think she exhausts Anna but I sure do enjoy that little girl's energy."

"Not so sure that Anna feels the same way," Miriam said lightly and both women laughed. It was no secret that Katie and Anna were often like oil and water, not mixing properly. With Katie's curiosity and energy, she often seemed to wear Anna's nerves thin.

The side door opened with a loud squeak and a bang as two men walked into the room. Hanging their battered straw hats on the hooks by the door, Elias and his son Steve stomped their boots on the doormat, kicking off some loose dirt, as they did every day before walking inside.

"Awful lot of laughter in here," the older man said. "Sounds like a real party. Are we menfolk invited?"

"Oh Daed," Mary Ruth said, rolling her eyes but unable to

hide her smile.

Elias walked over to his wife, placing his hand affectionately on her shoulder. He peered at the letter on the table. "Starting your circle letter, ja?"

"Indeed," Miriam replied. "I just finished it, in fact." Her eyes glanced over the piece of paper that was filled with her evenly spaced cursive writing. She had planned what to write for a long time and spent a good hour drafting the letter to make certain it was perfect. "I sure hope they write back soon. With all these people on the list, it could be at least two months before it gets back to us!"

"Sure hope you aren't expecting me to write no circle letter," Steve said, walking over to the large sofa by the back wall. He sat down and began to untie his boots. Kicking them off, he leaned back and shut his eyes. "Don't have nothing to write about, neither."

Shaking her head, Miriam frowned at her son. "You are not expected to write," she said sharply. "But you have plenty to contribute, so you better get on with it."

"Pphtt," he scoffed and waved his hand in her direction dismissively. "Work, work, work." He sighed, stretching his legs back. "And then, add in some more work," he added teasingly.

Ignoring him, Miriam turned back to the letter on the sturdy table in front of her. "Rachel is first on the list. I know she'll write her letter right quick. But Leah, now that's a different story." She paused, as a thought crossed her mind and tapped the letter with her finger. "Mayhaps I'll add a short note to Leah. I know how busy she can be with those *kinner*. But it would be a shame if she delayed the process." She glanced at her husband. "Even a short note is better than no note at all, ja?"

"I reckon," Elias said but his expression clearly showed that he didn't believe any note would help prod his daughter into action.

"Isaac's Anna is next," she continued.

Steve laughed. "She lives next door! You can just go ask her what's going on!"

Miriam set the list down and scowled at her son. "That's not the point! We share our letters with each other."

Tugging at his beard, Elias winked at his daughter as he said, "And you get to read those letters when Anna gets them, ain't so?"

"Elias!" Miriam gasped. "Are you accusing me of impatience?"

He laughed. "Not in the least!"

A loud noise interrupted the conversation. First they heard the sound of a car engine, screeching down the road followed by the noise of glass breaking. A lot of glass, it sure sounded like. Elias looked out of the window over the sink while Steve quickly pushed his feet back into his boots.

"The barn! It's from the barn!" Steve exclaimed as he jumped up on his feet and hurried toward the door.

Elias was right behind him but Steve was faster. "Be careful, son!"

Miriam shook her head, standing up and moving toward the door. "Be ready to call the police, Mary Ruth. Best dig out the number from the book on the desk."

For weeks, a group of young, rebellious teenagers had been vandalizing several farms in the area. A few days would pass with no incidents but then, the group would hit again. They threw rocks at the windows of barns and houses. Sometimes, they even broke buggy windows. It was unfortunate but no one had seen them yet, so the police couldn't stop them. And, just as the trail was getting warm, they would disappear for a while and all would return to normal.

By the time Miriam joined her husband and son outside,

Isaac had emerged from the dairy barn and Anna was hurrying across her front porch, young Katie at her heels. The younger *kinner* were already playing outside, clamoring around, eager to find out what the noise had been.

"How bad is it?" Miriam asked.

"Strangest thing," Elias said as he scratched his head and looked around. "Don't see no damage."

"We didn't imagine it," Isaac added, glancing up to nod at his younger brother, John David who joined them. He had been in the horse barn, apparently hitching his horse to the buggy to run a few errands before starting the afternoon chores.

"I sure heard the noise, Mamm!" Benjamin said as the six year old looked up at his mother, Anna. His eyes were wide and bright. Any kind of change in the daily routine was exciting to the six year old. This was no exception. "It was very loud!"

Anna placed her hand on his head, ruffling her fingers over his straight brown hair that was cut straight across his forehead and over his ears. She nodded as she replied, "I'm sure you did but I don't see no broken glass here."

"It's those bad men, ain't so?" Benjamin kicked at a rock on the driveway as if trying to prove he wasn't afraid of anyone.

"Now, now," Anna soothed, keeping her hand on his head.

For a long moment, no one knew what to say. They had heard the sound of the breaking glass but there was no sign that any window had been shattered. It was Steve who had the idea first. He looked up and glanced down the rest of the lane toward his own farm. It was situated directly across the street but hard to see through the trees.

"I wonder," Steve said slowly as he began to walk down the lane. The rest of the group caught the unspoken meaning and followed, quiet as they realized the fact that if the damage hadn't been at their own farm, it might very well have been at Steve's, right across the road.

Before they could even cross the street, they could see the broken windows. There it was: Shattered glass everywhere; in the grass, on the walkway and on the ledge. Two of the barn windows had been smashed. Since the windows were up high, it was impossible to see if there was any damage on the inside so Steve quickly hurried across the road and around the side of the barn to assess the damage.

There were two big rocks lying on the ground inside the barn. One was in the aisle way and the other was beside one of the cows. Her head was bleeding and she leaned weakly against the metal bar that separated the pens, breathing heavily. Clearly that cow was in pain.

"Aw come on!" Steve mumbled, taking off his hat to wipe the sweat off his forehead. He sighed as he placed his hand on her flank. "She's a pregnant cow, too!" He glanced over his shoulder at his daed, his expression both concerned and stressed. "Can you have someone call the vet as well as the police, Daed?"

Twenty minutes later, the police were taking statements. There were police cars lining the road and a group of Amish standing in a small huddle nearby. Despite not having phones in their homes, the neighbors had quickly heard the story. The Amish grapevine was as powerful as any social media network and, within minutes, the community descended upon the farm to show their solidarity and support for one of their own.

"We are very sorry about this, Mr. Fisher ," the officer said sympathetically as he closed his notepad. He looked at the damaged windows. "We're doing whatever we can to catch these fellows. They just keep staying one step ahead of us, but eventually, I am certain that we will catch them."

"I sure hope so," Elias said sternly.

The police officer exhaled sharply and ignored Elias. He turned his attention back to Steve. "I suggest you go to Hostetler's

Farm Store off Route 340 for the glass. You can have them send the bill to the police department. We have a special fund set aside for helping you folks out with situations like this."

Steve nodded. "I'm familiar with Hostetler's," he said solemnly. "What about the cow?"

The officer nodded. "Same thing. Vet bill to the police department." He sighed as he clicked the pen shut and slid it into his left front pocket. "Just wish these folks would leave your peaceful community alone."

"At least they aren't burning barns no more. That was bad, a few years back," Elias said as he looked over at his wife. "Wasn't it your nephew whose *fraa* lost a baby when their barn burned down?"

Miriam nodded. "Stillborn because of it, ja." She shook her head. "Poor Shana, she was heartbroken."

For a long moment, no one spoke, a moment of silence for the lost baby. The officer seemed uncomfortable, shifting his weight until he finally cleared his throat, the noise breaking the silence. "Well, I best get back and start filing this report. Too much time spent with paperwork," he said solemnly. "Eventually we'll catch these vandals. In the meantime, please be extra vigilant." He glanced over at the *kinner*. "Call us at the first sign of a speeding car and keep the little ones away from the road…just in case."

Anna shuddered, pulling Benjamin closer to her, protecting him from the thought of something awful happening to him or to one of her other children.

Little Katie stared with round eyes at the police car in the driveway. It was parked in the shadows of the barn. She watched as it drove away, the lights upon its roof no longer flashing red and blue. She was relieved when it was gone. She didn't like when the Englischers came to the farm. She much preferred the peace and quiet of the farm when she didn't have school and could help her mamm with the chores, just like this morning when they had been making cheese together.

Of course, she thought as she turned around and headed back toward the farmhouse, there was that one Englischer woman, the one from a place called the Big Apple, which she didn't mind too much. She had been at the farm a few weeks back, looking to board some ponies and horses. What was her name, Katie wondered as she stomped up the porch stairs.

Eleanor. Eleanor Haile.

Katie often heard her mamm call her just Ellie but Katie knew that it was short for Eleanor. She liked that name and often thought that, if she could, she would one day name one of her own daughters that pretty Englischer name. *Eleanor.*

She was as Englische as Englischers get, wearing blue jeans and cowboy boots. Sometimes she drove a shiny red pickup truck, other times a small blue car with four doors and a funny flag looking emblem on the wheels. With long brown hair and a big smile, this Eleanor had a lot of energy. She didn't treat Anna or Katie or any of her brothers and sisters as if they were some strange creatures like other Englischers sometimes did. Nor did Eleanor ask a lot of personal questions. She treated them like… well…people. And that's what Katie liked about her.

This Eleanor would pop in from time to time, usually on her way into town to visit some Mennonite relatives on the other side of Lancaster. She never called in advance although she always promised to do so when she'll be coming back. She would knock at the kitchen door, waiting patiently for Mamm to welcome her to their home. The good thing about Eleanor was that she talked to everyone, not just Mamm. She always took the time to speak to all of Katie's brothers and sisters, asking them about school or fishing or working the market stand, up the street. But the best thing about Eleanor was that she seemed to sparkle and glow when she spoke to Katie.

Just the other week Eleanor had been at the farm and stayed just long enough to help make some cookies before sitting down for a nice, cold glass of meadow tea. Eleanor had noticed all of Katie's toy animals lined up on the sofa. Immediately, Eleanor had realized that Katie had been playing schoolhouse. Without a bit of hesitation, Eleanor had sat down on the sofa, asked the names of the "students" and what subjects were their favorites.

Little Benjamin had laughed and stated the obvious. "Aw, they can't learn nothing! They's just stuffed toys!"

Eleanor had picked up the grey rabbit and flopped him on her lap, turning him over as if inspecting him. "Seems like a wise rabbit to me!" she said before gently placing the rabbit back on the sofa next to the stuffed bear. With a friendly wink at Katie, she turned back to Benjamin. "Maybe book learning is doing him some good!"

At that, Benjamin had made a sour face. "Book learning for a toy! That's silly!"

"Now, now," Mamm had said, opening the oven to pull out the cookies. The kitchen began to take on a lovely smell and Katie remembered her mouth watering. She loved cookie-making day even better than when Mamm baked bread. "Ellie, come have some meadow tea and try these freshly baked cookies," Mamm had said, "They are just out of the oven".

Mamm had continued to work while Eleanor moved over to the kitchen table. She pushed aside the weekly paper, The Budget, that was littering the bench, in order to make room for herself. "Anna," she had said. "Wanted to ask you a question."

"Ja?"

Eleanor had sipped at the glass of cold tea. "Boy, that's really good!"

Anna had laughed. "It's just meadow tea, Ellie! And that's

not a question."

"You're right," Eleanor had replied. "It's not the question. But you sure make the best tea that I've ever tasted, second only to Miriam's!" After setting the glass down on the table, she had glanced around the kitchen before continuing. "My husband needs to board some horses and ponies for about nine months. After our summer camp program, we just don't need them until the following June."

At the word "ponies", Katie had suddenly lost interest in the stuffed rabbit that Eleanor had touched and she moved over to the table, instead.

Anna had looked up. "Boarding? How many?"

Eleanor had shrugged her shoulders, in a free and graceful movement. Katie was mesmerized. She couldn't remember ever seeing her mamm shrug her shoulders. After all, her mamm was always too busy milking cows or washing clothes or cooking food or making cheese. Her mamm was just always too busy, period.

"Twenty or so."

"Oh my!" Anna had exclaimed. "I reckon that's too many for most farms. Not certain I know of anyone."

And that had ended the conversation about ponies and horses.

Now, as Katie plopped down on the torn blue sofa in the kitchen, she reached over with her arm to scoop up the toy rabbit from the floor where she had dropped it that morning. She held the rabbit in her lap and stared at it. She wondered how Eleanor had seen the magic in the rabbit when so many others missed it. Truly Eleanor was a special Englischer and Katie couldn't wait until she would return.

"You need to clean up those toys, Katie," Anna said as she walked into the kitchen, her eyes glancing over at the animals, books, and puzzle pieces that littered the floor. She frowned disapprovingly. "Floor looks real messy. We need a bit more order in here, I'm thinking."

"Why'd those boys do it, Mamm?"

Anna hurried over to clear the plates from the kitchen table. There were left over from that morning. "Don't you fret none more about those boys."

"They're Englischer boys, ain't so?" Katie asked.

Anna paused and looked out the window. Katie knew that her constant questions got under mamm's skin but she couldn't help herself. She wanted to know the answers. "Yes, Katie. Amish boys wouldn't be driving and certainly wouldn't be destroying people's property."

"Why then?"

With a sigh, Anna turned around. "Why what?" She pointed at the mess. "And you can pick up those toys while you're asking me these questions, ja?"

Katie scrambled off the sofa and began to scoop the toys into her hands in order to carry them to the crate in the other room. "Why do Englischers do such things but you said Amish boys wouldn't?"

"Our *kinner* are just raised different, I reckon," Anna answered. But Katie could tell that it wasn't a good enough answer.

"What about Eleanor?"

At the mention of her Englische friend, Anna laughed. "What about Eleanor? She has nothing to do with those bad boys!"

"But she's an Englischer. Surely she was raised in a similar way?"

This time, Anna hesitated. Clearly she could follow Katie's logic. That much was obvious from her expression. Katie waited patiently for an explanation. "*Ach, vell,*" Anna began. "Not all

Englischers are raised the same way."

"Nor are all Amish boys, ain't so?"

Taking a deep breath, her mamm shook her head. "You just have to trust me on this one, Katie. Eleanor is not like them and she was not raised like them. She's a *wunderbarr gut* friend to the family. Has been for many years, now."

"Ain't it true that *Onkel* James was sweet on her?"

Anna gasped. "Katie Fisher ! Where did you hear such nonsense?" She gestured toward the toys. "Enough of this chatter and you get those toys put away. Then outside you go. See if your daed needs some help. I'm through with these questions!"

Frowning, Katie hurried about her assigned chores. She could sure tell that her mamm was, indeed, finished with questions. Whenever she used her full name, Mamm meant business. There was no testing the water with her mamm when addressed in such a formal matter.

And so Katie went on with her assignment then helped her daed with the barn chores. After the evening meal, she went to bed early and slept straight through the night.

It was the following morning when Steve arranged for a car service to take him to the Hostetler's Farm Store. He didn't own a horse and a buggy. On the rare occasions when he used one, he always borrowed Isaac's. It wasn't as though he went many places so hiring a paid driver was the most economical and least time consuming way to go.

The cow had come through all right, requiring some stitches and antibiotics. The vet had said she was lucky. A few inches to the right and the cow would have suffered brain damage and most likely would have needed to be put down. Thank *Gott* for small blessings, he thought. Losing the one cow would have been a financial setback, not just for the loss of the daily milk she provided for the family but for the calf that she carried.

The bell at Hostetler's door jingled as he walked inside. It was an old building with a creaky wood plank floor and dusty shelves. A few kerosene lights hung overhead, from the old weathered beams, hissing as they cast a dim light throughout the store. Steve knew better than to look up at the flame. Doing so would cause instant blindness for a few seconds and black dots in his vision for a minute or more. While they might be dim, those lights were strong.

"May I help you?"

He turned in the direction of the soft yet cheerful voice, surprised to see a young Amish woman behind the counter. She wore a green dress with her black apron and white prayer *kapp*. Her face looked freshly scrubbed and young with the exception of the slight scar just over her right eyebrow and wrinkles under her hazel eyes. Yet, she looked familiar. "Uh…ja," he stammered, trying to remember why he was there. "Windows. I need two new windows for my barn."

"Oh ja," she said, nodding her head. "The police called Daed and said you might be here today. Heard about your barn. Feel really sorry about it"

"Your daed?"

"Jonas Hostetler," she responded, reaching beneath the counter for a pad of paper. "The owner."

He searched his memory for just a moment. There was something there. Was it a wedding? About ten years ago? He had been just twenty-four years old and paired up with a young woman who had amazingly similar eyes as the beautiful creature standing right before him. Only, he remembered, that he hadn't realized it then. Curious, Steve leaned against the counter. "You live by the Riehl farm, ja? Mimi Hostetler?"

"That's what my friends call me, ja?" Those hazel eyes met

his and narrowed for just a moment. "Do I know you?"

"Steve Fisher ," he said. "We had fellowship at a wedding once."

"We did?" Her voice sounded surprised. Her eyes flitted back and forth, taking in his face as if stretching back in her own memory. Clearly, she hadn't remembered him.

"I think so, anyway," he mumbled and stood straight. If he was a little disappointed that she didn't remember him, he did his best to hide it. After all, he scolded himself, it was ten years ago. Chances were that she was married with a pack of her own *kinner* at home. Although, he thought, if she was married, why would she still be working for her daed?

"About those windows," he said.

"Ja, ja…" she replied, bending her head back down. "Such a shame that those Englischer boys have such a penchant for mischief." She shook her head as she wrote something on a pad of paper. "They sure do have plenty of time to spare for doing nothing but trouble."

"Good hard farm work would solve that problem," Steve admitted.

She laughed and looked up at him. The sound was musical to his ears. So light and airy. And her eyes sparkled. "Good hard farm work solves a lot of problems, ain't so?" Looking up, she smiled. "That's what my daed tells me every morning at breakfast."

At breakfast? All of a sudden, Steve felt his heart quicken. Was she trying to tell him something? If she was having breakfast with her daed in the morning, certainly she wasn't married yet! But those eyes, he thought. How could such a beauty with such sparkling eyes and an angelic laugh not have captured someone's heart? "Your daed's a farmer?"

Another laugh escaped her lips. "*Nee*," she said lightly. "I just told you that he runs this store. But he keeps reminding me that there is great value in a strong farmer man," she added, the color immediately flooding to her cheeks. "Anyway, what size are those windows?" She took the measurements and made a note on the paper. Then, looking up at him, she gave him a final smile. "Was nice to see you again, Steven Fisher . We'll have those windows delivered with your brother Isaac's order for hay in two weeks."

He returned the smile and backed away from the counter. He wished there was something else to say but he knew that the conversation was over. Still, there was something about Mimi Hostetler. That dark hair and those pretty eyes lingered in his memory long after he slid back into the passenger seat of the car that had been waiting outside to take him back to the farm.

Mary Ruth sat on the porch, a plastic cup of fragrant meadow tea in her hand. Her mamm made the best meadow tea, although Anna's sure came close. Mamm's tea was never too sweet or weak. She seemed to use the right amount of tea from the garden every single time she made it. Try as Mary Ruth would, she could never replicate her mamm's recipe. She'd forget to take the leaves out or the water would boil over. Cooking just didn't seem to be her thing.

It was warm outside and she was still tired from the past few days cutting hay with her daed. Early mornings, long days and late nights were taking a toll on her. Now, with the sun shining and a warm breeze hitting her face, she shut her eyes and leaned her head back against the side of the house. *Why me*, she thought bitterly. Just when everything was going so well!

She knew that she shouldn't complain. After all, it had only been yesterday when her brother Steve's farm had been vandalized. He had been extra quiet during the morning milking, barely speaking to anyone. Although Steve was always soft-spoken and reserved, it was clear that he was disturbed by the invasion from the outside. Mary Ruth hated to see him upset. He was such a kind, gentle man. To see Steve upset truly bothered her.

Shortly after the morning chores, a car had pulled into the driveway. Mary Ruth had looked out the kitchen window, not surprised to see that Steve had disappeared with the Mennonite that he always hired to take him places. Letting the white curtain fall back over the glass, Mary Ruth could only presume that he had gone to the store to order the new windows. Steve was never one to let grass grow under his feet when it came to tending his farm, that was for sure and certain.

For the past few months, she had been traveling to the market down in Maryland to help her sister Sylvia and her husband John with their new meat stand. Traveling to market meant early morning rising and late nights coming home. The long days wore on her nerves, as did the funny things that the Englischers said and did. Oh, to be certain, she had gotten used to the surprising ways of the Englischers but had always known them to be simply curious about the Amish, never really malicious. Now that she had seen the other side of the Englischers' world, the dark side of mischief and vandalism, she realized there was more than met the eye to the world outside of Lancaster County. It worried her that anyone could be so hateful and mean spirited that they'd deliberately damage another person's property.

Despite all of that, however, it was the news that her mamm had sprung on her as they were preparing dinner for the men that left her stunned.

Mary Ruth took a short, crisp breath and opened her eyes. The fields were growing but it still would be weeks before the harvest. In the meantime, between Steve and John David, Isaac didn't need any help with the hay cutting coming up in two weeks. So, there was no excuse for Mary Ruth to say no to her sister Leah. She had just had a baby, after all, and needed the help. Even though their oldest sister Rachel lived on the adjacent farm, Rachel had her hands full with six *kinner* of her own. She couldn't spare the time or the hands to help Leah with this new baby...a special needs baby, at that.

"Don't like babies," she mumbled to herself.

She knew it was close to blasphemy but it was true. She had never warmed up to babies and didn't care one bit for having some of her own. She knew the hard work that went into being a farmer's wife and a mother to ten children from watching her own mamm. There was an endless amount of clothes to wash, food to cook, plates to shelve, and people to clean up after. Not for me, she told herself.

Now, Leah had asked for Mary Ruth to come visit and help her with this new baby. Her parents had said yes without even consulting her. Of course, Mary Ruth knew that, had they asked, she would have acquiesced. That was just what she did. She always said yes to help others, even when she wanted to run the other way.

It wasn't the farming life that bothered her. No, that wasn't it, for sure and certain. Cutting hay, plowing fields, and tending to the animals was right up there with Mary Ruth's favorite things to do. She loved working alongside nature and her family. She loved the smell of freshly turned earth. She loved the feel of the sun on her face. All of those things made her feel closer to God. After all, God wanted people to be proper stewards of the earth, to tend the soil and live from the land.

What bothered Mary Ruth was the idea that having ten or more children would keep her tied to the house. It wasn't even an idea. It was the expectation. She saw too many women getting married and, within ten months, having their first baby. For most young Amish wives, a new baby would come every 18 to 24 months. The house would become messy, the mother always tired and worn out, and the days of working the farm just plain over. And that was the real problem.

Even her sister-in-law, Anna, was a perfect example. Despite just moving to the main house, now that they had so many *kinner*, it was a mess. The kitchen was always filled with dirty dishes and the floor constantly needed a thorough washing. The children left toys everywhere and the counter was never cleared. Why? Because she had five small children and, from the looks of it, another one on the way.

"You thinking about packing then?" Miriam said as she opened the kitchen door. She stared at her daughter as she sat on the porch. Softening her voice, she added, "It will only be for a few weeks, Mary Ruth."

"Do I have to go?" Mary Ruth whined, immediately ashamed of herself. At twenty-one years of age, she should know better than to question her parents. Respect for one's parents was paramount to the Amish, second only to church and God. Despite the fact that she had been baptized last autumn, she still felt disconnected from the obligations that came along with it. Leaving her home to help her sister seemed to her quite a big stretch of the Golden Rule.

"Mary Ruth Fisher !" her mamm scolded. Her hands curled into fists, which she placed firmly on her wide hips.

As soon as her mother used her full name, Mary Ruth knew she was in trouble. "I'm sorry, Mamm," she mumbled.

"You should be!" Miriam snapped. "Your sister is in need of your help. She has a new *boppli* to tend to along with her other *kinner*. Not to mention that baby Jacob has special needs with that Down Syndrome. He has just as much need for love and family as the rest, maybe more so. God has blessed your sister Leah with a special challenge and we, her family, will be there to help her."

"Ach, Mamm," Mary Ruth said, shaking her head. "You know how I feel about babies."

Miriam raised an eyebrow at her youngest child. "Babies in general or this baby in particular?"

"In general!" Mary Ruth snapped. She knew what her mother was insinuating and it didn't please her. She wasn't avoiding helping Leah because the baby was different. That wasn't it at all. The truth was that she didn't like babies, clear and simple. And she didn't want to change her routine. Being home, helping with the farm work, and going to market with John and Sylvia was the pattern she liked to follow. Staying with Leah and living in her messy house was not something to look forward to.

"I don't appreciate that tone," Miriam said sternly, her eyes narrowing as she stared at Mary Ruth. "Now, it will do you good to get your bag packed. Your daed will be taking you there in the morning after milking time. And I expect nothing less than cooperation and help from you. This is your sister and her *kinner* that are in need."

And, with that, the discussion was over. Mary Ruth knew that she could never argue with both her daed and mamm. Once unified, it was a front that could not be conquered. To Leah's she was destined to go. And to help Leah with her *kinner* and baby Jacob was what she would have to do. She sighed as she stood up. *Best tackle it head on*, she thought, as she headed inside the house and proceeded to stomp upstairs to get her bag packed, hoping that the loud noise properly expressed her frustration. It was going to be a long few weeks, that was for sure and certain.

It was the next day, long after Elias had left in the buggy to take Mary Ruth over to Leah's farm that Miriam noticed the envelope sitting on the counter. She sighed and shook her head. *How many times,* she thought, *did I tell that girl to take the letter with her?* She glanced around the room, knowing that both Steve and John David were already busy in the barn, probably cleaning equipment from the morning milking.

Wiping her wet hands on her apron, Miriam picked up the letter that was addressed to her daughter, Rachel. Since she lived across the road from Leah, it would have been faster if Mary Ruth had taken the letter but she had forgotten. Now, there was only one way to get it there: the mailbox.

Miriam shook her head, disappointed that the journey of the circle letter was already delayed. With a quick glance at the clock, she realized that she still had time to get the letter to the mailbox in time for a morning pick-up. Luck might be on her side and the letter could possibly arrive the next day…two at the most.

Not bothering to put on her shoes, she hurried out of the kitchen, the screen door slamming behind her. The cows lifted their heads from the tall, green grass as she passed them in the fields. Miriam didn't seem to notice their inquisitive stares as she walked down the lane toward the mailbox at the end of the driveway.

Chapter Two: Rachel's Letter

Dear Family,

I was surprised to receive Mamm's letter but excited to begin writing. It will be wunderbaar gut to hear from my brothers and sisters. With the summer haying underway, we don't have much time for visiting much anymore. I'll be looking forward to Leah's church service in October when we all come together for worship and fellowship.

Elijah has recovered from his spring cold. Took him longer than we thought to get better. Thankfully, neighbors helped with the plowing and planting while he was recuperating.

The kinner are doing well. Lydia is taking her instructional and will be baptized this fall. We suspect our first wedding will follow shortly thereafter. But she hasn't said much more than asking about how much celery we planted last spring.

The boys' campout is being held at Menno Yoder's this Thursday and Friday. Elam and Nathan are excited to attend. It's the first campout for both since Nathan missed it last year due to his broken arm. I heard the boys are planning a softball game. I heard Menno is cutting hay early just so that the boys can have a good field to play in. Let's hope it doesn't rain as it has in past years.

Church was held at Alvin Zooks' yesterday. We had lots of visitors attend, including sister Mary Ruth. I know that Leah sure does appreciate her help with her kinner. It's a blessing to have an extra pair of hands while she is adapting to the boppli Jacob's needs.

We were saddened to hear about brother Steve's farm. We pray for the Englischers to stop those responsible before someone gets hurt. Fortunately, we have not had such experiences in our area.

Well, I have about 20 chickens to pluck and dress this afternoon so I best stop the letter writing for now. I will pass the letters along to sister Leah. With Mary Ruth at the farm, lending a hand as she is, Leah has no excuses for holding up the circle!

While I know it will be quite a few weeks, I also look forward to receiving updates about your families. May God keep and protect you and your families.

With much blessings,

Rachel

Squinting in the dim light of the room, Rachel reread her letter one last time before she folded it neatly and tucked it into a fresh envelope. She took Mamm's original letter and the list of addresses from the old envelope and slid these inside, too. Then, raising the envelope to her lips she quickly licked the glue in order to shut it.

"Nathan!" she yelled out. "Nathan? Where are you?"

"Here, Mamm." Her sixteen-year-old son poked his head around the corner from the washroom. "What you need?"

"Be needing you to run this over to Leah's mailbox," Rachel said as she stood up. She waved the envelope in the air as if beckoning him to take it. "We all know how long it takes for her to respond so the sooner she gets it, the better for the others."

"Aw Mamm," he whined, making a face. "It's so hot out!"

Rachel frowned. "No back talk, now! Or I'll be telling your daed and there will be no campout for you."

Grumbling under his breath, Nathan slowly walked over to his mother and took the letter. "Just to the mailbox, right?"

"Might be nice if you stopped in to say hello," she replied, turning her back to her son as she assessed the kitchen. The dinner dishes still needed to be put away and she had a long afternoon of folding the freshly laundered clothing that hung on the line to dry. Lydia was gone visiting friends for the afternoon and the smaller *kinner* were playing outside. Once Lydia returned, they'd tackle the chickens and get them ready for market.

Glancing out the window, she watched as Nathan sluggishly made his way down the lane. Her other son, Elam, emerged from the barn and hurried to catch up, skipping alongside his brother. It was a mile walk to Leah's. It was *gut* that he would have company although she reckoned she had a good hour before they would be back. Certainly they'd stop in to visit with the *kinner* and to see if Leah had any of her famous fresh baked shoo fly pie. Without doubt, Leah made the gooiest and tastiest shoo fly pie in their entire church district. Whenever there was a bake sale, her shoofly pies were always the first to sell out.

The clouds began to thicken and the sky turned darker. Rachel wondered if it might rain after all. She decided to tackle the laundry first to be on the safe side. The dishes could wait to be put away, but if it rained, the laundry would get soaked and that would create more work for her.

Outside on the porch, she pulled at the clothing line. The big round wheel squeaked as it moved. She made a mental note to mention it to Elijah. Would do no good if it rusted, that was for sure and certain. Too expensive to replace it.

The air was muggy and some of the clothes still felt damp. She set them to the side, knowing that they'd have to finish drying inside the house. The sky was growing darker and a breeze blew in. Indeed, the rain was on its way. Rachel could feel it, the humidity in the air, the subtle scents emanating from her garden as the plants were opening up to soak in their liquid nourishment. She hoped it would pass quickly so that the field would dry out for the campout planned at the Yoder's. Muddy fields meant dirty clothing and, if the rain didn't stop, sick boys. With haying just another week away, that would not help Elijah one bit.

She sighed as she removed Elam's pants off the line. There was a hole over the right knee that she had already patched a couple of weeks before. *Something else to fix,* she thought as she made a mental note to ask her husband to pick up another set of wooden clothespins from the store. Instead of doing the laundry just on Mondays as was before, it now had to be done twice a week, sometimes even three times with all the *kinner* around. She glanced over toward the barn where Jonas, Rachel Ann, and Sarah were playing with the kittens. "You best be coming in," she called out, "It's going to storm anytime, now."

As they hurried toward the porch, she stopped Sarah before she dashed inside. "Want you to sweep the kitchen floor and get Rachel Ann to put away all these dinner dishes."

"Yes, mamm," Sarah said.

The rain began to fall, immediately after; slowly at first. Rachel hurried and began pulling the clothes off the line. She could fold them and put them away later. She just didn't want more work with wet clothing. Already, the washroom was going to be a mess from the chickens. To have wet clothes hanging everywhere! She sighed again. There was nothing that she disliked more than a disorderly house. She liked her house clean and things put away. Cleanliness was next to godliness, after all.

She had just pulled the last piece of clothing off the line when a streak of lightening flashed through the sky. A few seconds later, she heard the crack. "Going to be a doozey," she mumbled and hurried into the house, the wooden screen door slamming shut behind her. At least they needed the rain and they weren't going to hay until next week. If it rained now, the fields would most likely be dry in time for cutting and baling. Once cut, rain could ruin the hay. Damp hay couldn't be baled since there was always the risk of mildew or, even worse, fire in the barn. Damp hay smoldered and burned many a barn each summer; not to mention what moldy hay could do to the animals, causing colic and possibly death if ingested in large quantities.

The rain began pelting against the windows, the noise reverberating throughout the kitchen. It was soft at first then louder. She stood by the table and continued separating and folding the laundry. Most of it had been pulled off the line in time.

Dressing chickens was most likely not going to happen, she realized. With a sigh, she quickly changed her course of action for the afternoon. Corn flake sugar cookies, she thought. I'll have the *kinner* help me make corn flake sugar cookies. If everyone was going to be trapped inside the house, a fun afternoon of cookie making would suit just fine and cheer up some moods.

"Jonas, you best be lighting the lanterns," she said over her shoulder. "Too dark to see much with the storm and all."

Obediently, her son nodded and hurried over to the wall where the matches hung by the strike pad. He fished inside for a match and was just about to strike it when Rachel heard noise coming from outside. It was loud enough to be heard over the increasing downpour. She bent down and looked out the window but couldn't see anything. A frown creased her forehead and she hurried over to the door. As she opened it and stepped onto the porch, she heard it clearly.

"Mamm!"

Elam was screaming and calling out her name. Her heart started to pound inside of her chest. Something bad must have happened. She started to run off the porch to head in the direction from which he was calling her, but before she got to the bottom step, she saw him running around the barn. He was wet and out of breath.

"Lord, child! Slow down!" she called.

She didn't want to see him fall on the wet grass. But he continued to run. His eyes were wild and his skin pale. She reached out to take him in her arms when he bounded up the porch steps. He collapsed against her, his heart racing as he tried to catch his breath.

"You need to go to Leah's!"

"What is it?" A thousand thoughts raced through her mind. Clearly something had happened. Was it the baby? "Calm down," she asked as she placed her hands on his shoulders. "Take a deep breath and tell me what happened." She sounded calmer than she felt. She had to.

"There was an accident," he gulped.

Rachel gasped. "At Leah's?"

Elam shook his head. "*Nee*, not at Leah's. At the Yoder's, next door."

For a moment, she couldn't understand what he was saying. The neighbors had an accident? Why would Elam be running to her? Certainly it couldn't be that bad. "The Yoder's?" she asked, more for clarification.

He stared up at his mamm. "Menno's *fraa*...she's dead!" Elam spurted with welling eyes.

Rachel's hand fluttered to her mouth. Dead? Dear Lord, she thought. Martha Yoder was so young, just thirty years old! They had children. Small children. No wonder Elam had come for her. Leah wouldn't be able to handle the situation in the least. With the storm, it would take time for the family members to be notified. No one would be checking the phones in their barn this evening.

"You stay with the *kinner*," she whispered and hurried out to the barn. She had to find Elijah and get over to Leah's immediately. They would need to help Menno Yoder get through this tragedy, whatever had happened. An accident and a death would mean a lot of time spent healing for many people in the community, but for tonight, Rachel wanted to see how she could help Menno with his *kinner* until his own mamm could get to the farm.

Once the buggy pulled up to Leah's barn, Rachel jumped out and ran into the house. Elijah hitched the horse to the side of the barn and followed, just a few seconds behind her. The *kinner* were crowded around the table, several of them weeping as they clung to each other and their mamm. Leah and Mary Ruth did their best to console them and, when Rachel walked in, both women looked thankful.

"It's awful," Leah said, jumping up to run to her older sister. She collapsed in Rachel's arms. Leah had always been the fragile one, the sister who was unsure of herself and emotional. Rachel had learned to deal with it a long time ago. "I don't know what to do!"

"Get a hold of yourself," Rachel said gently and held her sister at arm's length. Leah was crying, which only made the *kinner* sob, too. "For the little ones," she whispered. "Now, tell me what happened?"

"It was an accident with the baler."

That didn't make sense. "The baler?" Why would Martha be working a baler? In this weather? She glanced at her husband. He was pale and speechless.

Leah nodded, trying to stifle a sob. "Martha saw the rain coming and hurried out with her oldest boy to start baling the hay. They had cut it last week for the campout, you know."

Rachel was well aware of that. Nathan and Elam had been so looking forward to the overnight with their friends. Everyone knew that Menno had cut hay early to accommodate the boys, but when the rain swept through, Rachel had forgotten about the cut hay at the Yoder's farm. "Dear Lord," she whispered.

"The baler was wet, she slipped, and the machinery…it just crushed her," she said, lowering her voice. "Right in front of the boy."

"Melvin?" Rachel gasped. He was just a young boy, no more than ten. "We need to go over to them," Rachel said quickly. She glanced around. The *kinner* were still crying and Leah was clearly too upset to leave the house. *No help coming from her,* Rachel thought. Her eyes fell upon Mary Ruth who had her arms around Leah's daughter.

"Mary Ruth! Come with me," she insisted and hurried to the door. Glancing over her shoulder, she saw that Mary Ruth was merely staring at her, a blank expression on her face. "Come along now! We need to help Menno until his family can come to tend to his needs and the *kinner*."

There were five buggies in the driveway of the Yoder's farm. There was also an ambulance and two police cars, which looked terribly out of place at the Amish farm. Besides, Mary Ruth was tired of seeing police cars but she obediently followed her older sister as they hurried into the house.

The kitchen was dark. No one had thought to light a lantern yet. Menno was sitting at the table, his head in his hands. His face was blotchy and it was clear that he was still in shock. Mary Ruth hung by the door, uncertain why her sister had insisted that she'd accompany her. It wasn't as if she knew the Yoder's. But Rachel knew exactly what to do. She hurried over and lit the lanterns. Then she moved over to the three children who were weeping, sitting next to each other on the sofa. Rachel kneeled in front of them and pulled them into her arms, holding them and letting them sob against her shoulders. The youngest one was sucking on her thumb, a ratty stuffed bear in her arms.

Mary Ruth shuddered. From what she could tell, Menno and Martha had four children, one son and three daughters. They were young, ranging from four to ten. The ten-year-old was a boy and he sat on a chair in the other room, his eyes staring blankly at the floor. No one seemed to be paying any attention to him. Mary Ruth wondered if he was Melvin, the boy who had been with his mamm when she died. She suspected he was and she wished she knew what to do or say.

"This can't be. It makes no sense," the man said. His voice was soft and his eyes void of life. He was staring at nothing with his head bent down. "Martha can't be gone," he whispered.

An older man with a long white beard placed his hand on Menno's shoulder. "We cannot question the Lord for His reasons," he said. Mary Ruth recognized him as the bishop of Leah's church district. He had preached at the service just yesterday. "You will get through this, Menno. We will help you."

"Why?" he mumbled to himself. "Why Martha?" He looked up at the bishop. His eyes were now red and filled with tears. "Why?" He seemed to be pleading with the bishop for an answer, but when none came, he dipped his head back down and continued staring at the tabletop.

Mary Ruth glanced at the boy one more time. His thick curly hair was tucked behind his ears and his shirt was ripped at the shoulder. She wondered if that had happened after the accident. She imagined he had tried to save his mamm before he had run for help. She hated the fact that he was sitting alone, no one paying any attention to him. The smaller girls were being comforted by Rachel and the men were supporting Menno. But the boy was alone and in just as much need of consideration.

Taking a deep breath, she went over to his side. Kneeling before him, she touched his arm. His eyes flickered to look at her. They were dull and lifeless. All Mary Ruth could think about was this poor boy witnessing the death of his mother. He blinked his eyes once but said nothing in response to her.

"Let me get you something," she whispered. "Water, mayhaps?" She didn't wait to hear if he spoke. Instead, she hurried to the sink. She needed to be busy, to move around the kitchen. She had never witnessed such a solemn scene. It was as if a heavy cloud was hanging over the room, draining it of energy. It felt oppressive, as if a weight was pressing against her chest. She wished that she could leave, to get away from the sorrow and pain lingering in the air, but she knew that dealing with the wrath of Rachel would be worse than staying.

Please help this family, Lord, she prayed to herself. *Please help that child.*

"Don't touch that!"

Startled, Mary Ruth spun around at the sound of the stern, deep voice that boomed throughout the room. She was surprised to see that Menno had looked up, his dark eyes piercing and glaring at her. She realized that he was yelling at her for opening the cabinet to get a plastic cup. Her hand was inside the cabinet and she froze, uncertain whether to move away or to continue.

Menno continued to glare at her. "That's his mamm's job!" he snapped. "She tends her children, not you!"

"Menno," the bishop said gently, placing his hand on Menno's shoulder. "Mary Ruth is just trying to help." He nodded at Mary Ruth to continue. "Your boy's mamm is gone, Menno. Martha can't comfort Melvin now. But we are here to comfort all of you."

"That's his mamm's job," he repeated, this time his voice was softer, almost a resigned utterance.

Mary Ruth handed the drink of water to the boy. He took it but didn't drink it. Mary Ruth rubbed his back gently, wishing that she was more like Rachel, so confident and able to take charge. It felt awkward to comfort a child that she didn't really know. She had only met the Yoder family a few times at church functions with Rachel and Leah. She hadn't paid any attention to them. Now, she wished she had spent a moment getting to know Martha Yoder. But it was too late. She was gone and nothing could change that.

The funeral was held three days later. After all, it took three days to dig the grave, prepare the coffin, and arrange the house. Rachel insisted on helping as much as she could during that time, bringing food over to the house and making certain that the *kinner* were fed. Several times, she brought Mary Ruth with her, leaving Leah to care for the smaller children.

"Why me?" Mary Ruth asked. She dreaded going to the house.

Rachel frowned at her. "They need us" was her sister's simple answer.

With Rachel, there was no arguing. Mary Ruth had learned *that* years ago. As the oldest sibling of seven, Rachel had been taught to take charge from a small age. It was part of her upbringing and something that everyone had long ago come to depend upon. And as the youngest of seven (nine if you counted the two that died as babies), Mary Ruth had learned that her life was a constant stream of taking orders from those who were in charge.

During each visit, Mary Ruth busied herself cleaning the kitchen. There was a never-ending pile of dishes as people came by to sit with the body and to show support for Menno. Then, there was the viewing when Martha's body was laid out in the sitting room and the family gathered around to reflect and say their goodbyes.

Mary Ruth tried not to look into the room. She didn't want to see the coffin. It was a simple pine box and was kept shut. For that, Mary Ruth was grateful. She didn't want to see the body of Martha Yoder. Certainly Martha wore her wedding dress, a pale blue dress with a white apron. But her body had been badly maimed and the decision had been made by her family to not upset the community with a viewing that entailed witnessing her injuries.

After that viewing, four men had carried the pine box outside to the horse drawn carriage. It was a buggy with an open back, just long enough to support the coffin. Mary Ruth felt her throat swell as she watched Menno following the men, his children close behind. A long line of buggies drove along the road behind the buggy where the coffin laid. They were headed to the cemetery;

there the bishop would preach about the glory of God. There would be very little mention of Martha, just a simple reading of her name, birth date, and death date when he was finished preaching.

Mary Ruth stood next to Rachel and Elijah during the graveside preaching. Her eyes shifted from the hole in the ground which now contained Martha's coffin, to the pale, drawn face of Menno Yoder, still in shock over losing his young wife. When the family began to toss dirt into the hole, Mary Ruth felt tears falling down her cheeks and she had to look away. It was too much for her to handle. Death seemed a cruel aftermath to life, especially for such a young woman.

At least four hundred people showed up, each family bringing food and well wishes for the Yoders. But Menno sat by himself, ignoring the kind words. He didn't greet the people as he couldn't bring himself to talk with anyone. Instead, he stared ahead, his expression blank and seemingly void of emotion.

Mary Ruth glanced at him from time to time as she scurried about the kitchen. Since she didn't know the Yoders, she felt more comfortable helping Leah in the kitchen. Rachel had taken charge of the younger children, making certain that they were bathed and dressed proper to say goodbye to their mamm. Mary Ruth noticed that, once again, Melvin, the boy, was sitting by himself. No one seemed to be paying attention to him or concerned with his isolation and quiet demeanor.

"Has anyone talked to the older boy?" she whispered to Rachel when her sister hustled into the kitchen. For a moment, Rachel didn't seem to understand what Mary Ruth was asking. "Melvin," Mary Ruth prompted, her eyes flickering to where he sat. "Did anyone talked to him?"

Rachel looked around. "Where is he?" Her eyes fell onto the slumped figure of the ten year old. "Go talk to him, Mary Ruth."

"Me?" Mary Ruth didn't know what to say to a grieving ten-year-old. The last time she had tried to comfort him, his daed had cast such a horrible look her way. She could still hear his words booming in her ears. She certainly didn't want him yelling at her again, not with all of these people around.

"Say anything," Rachel hissed, nudging her in the boy's direction. "Unless you want to watch the smaller *kinner*."

With a sigh, Mary Ruth approached the small boy. He wore his black suit and hat but his head was dipped down so that she had to kneel before him in order to see his face. "Melvin," she said softly. When he didn't look at her, she reached out with a finger and touched his chin. Tilting his head back, she smiled gently at him. "Melvin, I'd like to fix you a plate to eat. You need some food."

He blinked.

He was a beautiful boy with long, dark eyelashes and a thick head of curly brown hair that flopped over his ears. His skin was the color of honey from having worked outside during the spring and summer days. But those eyes...so dark and chocolaty...were vacant. It broke her heart to see the pain on his face.

She glanced over at the room where the men were seated. Menno was surrounded by men in black suits. He, too, had the same vacant look. In fact, she realized as she stared at him, Melvin was a smaller version of Menno only with a much larger problem: A future without a mamm. Clearly, his daed was in no shape to tend to this child. And his mamm was gone.

Mary Ruth took a deep breath and reached down for Melvin's hand. "Melvin, I want you to come with me now," she said, trying to sound gentle but firm. To her surprise, his hand tightened around hers and he stood up. "That's a good boy," she whispered.

Leading him to the kitchen, she sat him down on a bench and hurried to fill a plate with food. Chicken, corn, potatoes, beans, and fresh bread. She figured that he hadn't eaten since yesterday and would be hungry. Setting the plate next to him on the bench, Mary Ruth knelt before him. "I don't know what you like, Melvin, but I put a little bit of everything on your plate. Is that OK?"

No response.

She touched his knee to reassure him then stood up. It was best if she left him alone, she figured. Too much smothering would have the opposite effect. He needed to grieve. After all, his mother had only died a few days ago. While Mary Ruth knew that she had gone home to the Lord, she also knew that it probably didn't seem like a fair trade to a ten-year-old facing a life without a mamm. But suddenly, she remembered.

He saw it happen!

A shudder went through her entire body as she thought, once again, about Melvin seeing his mamm slip from the baler and getting crushed under the weight of the equipment. She shut her eyes and shook her head, trying to push the vision away. It would take a long time for the family to recover from this loss but even longer for Melvin, she realized.

Steve wasn't certain why his mamm had insisted that he'd come to the funeral. He barely knew the Yoder family, being that they lived two church districts apart from their own. Menno was about his age, that much was true. But they hadn't run with the same youth group.

Mamm had argued that it was the right thing to do, especially with Rachel and Leah living next door. So, without arguing further, he had donned his Sunday suit and ridden over with his parents. He hated being crammed in the back of the buggy and, for the briefest of moments, wished he had his own to use. But the thought was fleeting. There was no need to have a buggy, not at this particular stage in his life.

Now, as he stood among the men, he felt the whole weight of the event upon him. *Death*, he thought. A bad thing for a young man with *kinner*. He took a deep breath and glanced around the room. He knew some of the men, especially the younger ones. Jonas Hostetler and Stephen Esh were nearby, standing awkwardly with their hands behind their backs as if they didn't know what to say or do.

"Sad day, ja?" Steve said as he approached them.

"That it is," Stephen Esh replied, bowing his head slightly. "But she's home with our Lord."

For a moment, Steve stared at Stephen Esh. His friend spoke as if being at home with the Lord was supposed to wash away the pain and grief. He wondered if Menno Yoder felt that way. Glancing over his shoulder, he stared at the man seated in the lone chair in the room. The crowd of men surrounding him appeared just as lost as Menno. No, Steve thought. I don't think Menno feels the glory of his wife being with the Lord yet.

But, rather than say that, Steve merely took a deep breath and nodded. "Ja, some comfort there, I'm sure," he said.

Three young women, dressed in black dresses with white aprons, walked by. As they did, Stephen Esh glanced at the taller of the two and gave a soft smile. Steve followed his gaze and, for the briefest of moments, he frowned. He recognized the one woman but couldn't place from where he knew her. Her eyes flickered toward Steve and he thought she recognized him, too. Yet, the crowd was too large and the situation too uncomfortable for Steve to pursue her and ask for her name.

Instead, he turned to Stephen and, with a nod of his head in the direction of the women, whispered, "Who was that?"

Stephen followed his gaze. When he saw the three women, the younger one looked back and smiled, a soft and appropriate smile, given the situation. "Ach, Priscilla? She's my girl." He paused. "Priscilla Smucker."

Steve shook his head. "*Nee*, the other one."

"*Vell*, that would be her older sister, Annie, and the other one is Annie's friend, Mimi Hostetler." He looked back at Steve and raised an eyebrow. "You know them?"

"*Nee*," he said. "Not directly. But I reckon I ran into Mimi at the store." He turned his attention back to his friends. "Had some vandals break a window in my barn. Needed to replace the glass."

"Ja, that would be her, then," Jonas said. For a moment, Jonas studied Steve's face. "She's my cousin, you know. On my mamm's side."

Steve tried to appear nonchalant. "You don't say, ja?"

"Works for her daed," he affirmed. Then, a sparkle in his eye, Stephen lowered his voice and whispered. "Nice girl. Ain't married, you know."

Steve leaned forward and lowered his own voice. "Ain't asking, you know."

The three men stifled a quiet laugh, too aware that this was neither the appropriate time nor place to be joking. After all, they had all come together to support Menno Yoder and his family as they celebrated the fact that, despite being missed after such an unfortunate tragedy, Martha Yoder now resided in the glory of the Lord.

Little Katie stood in the kitchen, her back against the wall. Her mamm was busy helping the other women and her older cousins were watching the younger children, keeping them occupied outside. But Katie didn't want to go outside. She wanted to be near her mamm. Ever since she had heard about the accident with Martha Yoder, Katie had barely let her mamm out of her sight.

She hadn't met Martha Yoder but she sure knew Melvin Yoder. A few times, Katie had been over at Leah's, playing with her cousins outside. Melvin had been there. After all, his daed's farm was right next door, just a stone's throw from the swing by the pond.

And that was what Katie thought about...Melvin witnessing his mamm getting killed by the baling machine. They were close in age so Katie found it easy to shut her eyes and imagine how he felt. There was only one word that could sum it up: *lost.*

Katie would feel lost without her mamm. Katie would feel lost among these people. Katie would feel lost with having been the last person to see her mamm smile and laugh...and breathe. Tears welled into her eyes and she fought the urge to cry. Turning her face away from the crowd, she leaned her forehead against the wall and squeezed her eyes shut. *I will not cry, I will not cry,* she told herself.

"Are you all right, Katie?"

The voice in her ear sounded so familiar. When she turned around, she was surprised to see her aunt, Mary Ruth. "Ja," she sniffled. "I'm fine." She had heard that Mary Ruth was staying with Leah. She had seen Mary Ruth fluttering around the kitchen and helping to wash dishes, clear plates, and tend to the needs of the guests. But she hadn't thought that Mary Ruth would notice her.

"You want to talk?"

"*Nee,*" Katie said, trying to put on a brave face. "I'm just fine," she repeated.

"You don't look fine," Mary Ruth said softly, leaning down to wipe the remnant of a tear from her face. "Mayhaps you should sit down for a spell, ja?" Without waiting for an answer, Mary Ruth took her arm and led her over to the place where Melvin sat. "Keep each other company in your sorrow," she whispered.

And then Mary Ruth was gone.

Katie sat next to Melvin, the one person in the room whom she did not wish to sit next to. She worried that she didn't know what to say to him and her words would get jumbled. She worried that her tears would upset him and that would surely get her in trouble with the adults, but even worse, she worried that death would be contagious and, Lord have mercy, strike her own mamm.

"You OK?" she said softly, surprised to hear the words come out of her mouth.

"*Nee*," he replied. A short and simple answer that expressed the dearth of despair in his heart. *Nee.*

"I'm terribly sorry about your mamm," she offered, forcing herself to lift her eyes and meet his sad gaze. She was afraid to look at him, afraid to be near him. What if his mamm's death was contagious? Still, despite her fears, she was drawn to Melvin and wanted to be a friend to him.

Melvin didn't seem to notice her reluctance. The little boy shrugged. "I'm supposed to be happy that she's with the Lord."

It sounded weak, even as he said it. They both knew it was the right thing to say, but neither could believe it.

"Are you?"

"Am I what?" he asked.

"Happy that she's with the Lord?"

He met her gaze. For the longest moment, he couldn't answer her. It seemed as though he was thinking but was gaining strength from both her question, her presence and her stare. Finally, he took a deep breath and exhaled. "*Nee*, Katie Fisher ," he said. "*Nee,* I'm not happy. In fact, I'm angry that the Lord would take my mamm away from me. I don't understand it and I don't understand what people are saying to me. I miss her." He paused and moved his eyes to stare down at his feet. Then, in the softest voice, almost inaudible, he whispered, "I want her back."

For a moment, she thought she hadn't heard him. She had to repeat the words to herself. *I want her back.* Katie chewed on her lower lip. Yes, she had heard him say those very words. Four simple words that said so much about how he felt. She didn't blame him. After all, that's how she figured she would feel if something horrible happened to her own mamm, even if she hadn't been there to witness it. Yes, she would certainly feel plenty confused, a lot bitter, and a whole heap of loneliness. She reached her hand out and touched his. To her surprise, he let her hold his soft hand in hers.

"Melvin Yoder," she said softly. "I do understand."

Rachel sat for a long time, sitting in her reading chair, an old plush rocking chair that creaked ever so slightly when it rolled backward. The kerosene lantern that hung overhead hissed as it flung its bright light throughout the room. On her lap was her Bible but she simply couldn't open it tonight. Instead, she just held it, feeling her strength return just from the mere touch of its worn, faded leather cover.

Her heart ached for the Yoder family. It had been a grueling few days. She shut her eyes and silently prayed for Menno and his children. It would be a rough road ahead of Menno, especially with small children that needed tending to. There would be laundry and cooking, gardening and canning. The community would help, as much as they could, that was for sure and certain. But it would still be very stressful for the family.

She was proud of Mary Ruth for having helped with the young boy. As the youngest child in the family, Mary Ruth was used to being taken care of, it seemed to Rachel…much more than caring for others. The compassion that Mary Ruth demonstrated at the Yoders was a small blessing in this sorrowful event.

She shut her eyes. Tomorrow was another day. Lydia would finally help her with the chickens and it was another laundry day. On a farm, there was never a break in the work routine. It continued, whether or not life stopped around it. At least it was something that could be counted on, she thought to herself. The routine of farm life, however demanding.

With a big sigh, she glanced over at her husband. He was seated in the chair next to her, the Budget newspaper in his hands. "Think I'll be turning in for the night, Elijah," she whispered. "Need a good night's sleep for tomorrow."

He nodded. "I'll be up shortly," he said. "Need to finish my reading."

She smiled. "You and your Budget!"

He smiled at her. "You have your circle letters to keep you in touch with everyone and I have my Budget to keep updated on plantings, crops, and other news."

Walking over to him, she placed her hand on his shoulder. He paused and looked up at her. Then, setting the paper down, he reached for her hand. For a long moment, he held it, staring at her. The only noises were the hiss from the kerosene lantern and the gentle ticking of the old clock on the wall. It had been a gift from Elijah to Rachel when there were married.

Rachel studied Elijah's face. It was weathered and wrinkled from working in the sun. Over the years, his beard had grown long enough to touch his chest and the brown hairs were now sprinkled with grey. But he was still the handsome man who used to court her with a sparkling new buggy, one that caused the bishop to raise an eyebrow while the community wagged their tongues.

"It was a tough few days," she whispered.

He nodded his head but he didn't speak.

"I'm not going anywhere," she said softly.

He shut his eyes as he gave another stiff nod of his head. "Don't," he replied. He looked up at her then, his eyes tired and concerned. She realized that he, too, had been affected by Martha Yoder's death. He tried to act stoic and strong, but in that moment, she saw that he had visualized himself in Menno's place. Clearly, the thought had left him frightened, but as soon as she saw the concern in his face, he released her hand and, as he cleared his throat, Elijah turned his attention back to the Budget.

Rachel could tell that he wasn't reading. Perhaps he hadn't been reading at all that evening. It touched her that he, too, was so wrapped up in the tragedy that had befallen the Yoder family. It was comforting to know that she was not alone in feeling fear in God's decision to take Martha Yoder home at such a young age. She also suspected that, like her, Elijah was also praying for guidance on how to help that family through the upcoming weeks and months.

With a deep breath, she set her Bible on the seat of her chair and turned to leave the room. The Yoder family suffered, but alongside them, the entire community was feeling their pain. It would take a long time for them to heal and move on with their lives. Of that, she was sure and certain.

Chapter Three: Leah's Letter

Dear Family,

With so much happening in our district, I near forgot to write. Sister Rachel was kind enough to remind me several times this week that I needed to write a letter and continue the circle letter. Figured I best do it before a fourth reminder came my way.

Mary Ruth has been such a blessing to us, helping not just with the kinner while I tend to Jacob's needs but helping with the Yoder family as they adjust to life without Martha.

Rachel set up a community schedule for women to help with the daily chores, especially cooking. Mary Ruth has been taking the kinner during the day. Between watching my Elmer, Edna, Emma, and Caleb as well as the Yoder kinner, she sure has her hands full. I'm pleased to see such a motherly instinct developing in her after all.

Church Sunday is only three weeks away and I'm sure looking forward to having the entire family here. Jonah has been working from before sunrise to well after sunset to make certain the barn is fixed and proper. It's too hot to have the service in the house. He also has to cut and bale the hay before then, something we are all apprehensive about these days, given the terrible accident at Yoder's farm.

Was sorry to hear about the vandalism at Steve's farm. I sure hope that cow is better and the window fixed. Such sad times that we live in.

Not much else to add to the news so I will send the letter onto James' Lizzie so that I'm not holding up the circle anymore.

May the good Lord bless each of you and your families.

Leah

Leah tossed the pen onto the table and quickly folded the letter. She shoved it into an envelope and pushed in the other two letters, the one from Rachel and the original one from Mamm along with the list of addresses. She didn't care if they crinkled. *Get this out of here so Rachel stops asking me about it*, she thought as she licked the envelope and dropped it on the table. She'd ask Elmer to run it to the mailbox later that evening. She just hoped that she wouldn't forget.

Circle letters, she thought. Who has time for writing letters, especially since everyone would be at her house in just a few short weeks! She had far too much to do with tending to the house, the garden, and baby Jacob. His needs were so great and her time was too short for such trivial things as letters. Silly idea, she told herself as she stood up and hurried over to the kitchen to start preparing for the noon meal. Jonah would be hungry, that was for sure and certain. He had been cleaning the barn all morning, even after tending to the cows.

Leah sighed and looked out the window over the kitchen sink. Truth was that Jonah had been spending a lot more time in the barn, period. *Ever since Jacob had been born*, she thought wryly. It didn't take much for her to realize that Jonah was none to pleased with his special needs baby, a son at that. He rarely helped the baby, never spoke to him, and just didn't seem to acknowledge that the baby excited.

Prayer hadn't helped, that was for certain. Leah prayed constantly for the strength to cope with this challenge. Yes, Jacob had that Down Syndrome. Yes, it was one of the more extreme cases that the doctors had seen. But God was good and never gave more than people could handle. Leah believed that with her entire heart.

There were footsteps on the porch and Leah looked up as Mary Ruth hurried into the mudroom from outside. "Headed over to Yoder's then, are you?" she called out.

"Ja," Mary Ruth replied, her voice flat and emotionless.

"You take that shoofly pie now, you hear?" *After all,* Leah thought, *I only got up extra early to make it for the Yoder family. Leave it to Mary Ruth to forget it.*

"Ja," Mary Ruth said, this time with a tone to her voice.

"I'll send the *kinner* when they are done with their meal," Leah added, ignoring Mary Ruth's testiness and spiteful glare. There was nothing for her younger sister to be upset about, she told herself. Helping others was God's calling. That's what community did…helped each other during time of crisis. Leah only wished there were far fewer crisis in the community these days.

Reluctantly, Mary Ruth walked along the road that headed to Menno Yoder's farm. It was more direct and much quicker to cut through the field, that was true, but she wasn't looking for either direct or quick. Not today. Each footstep felt heavy and burdensome, as though she was carrying a great weight down the road, not just a freshly baked shoofly pie.

She wasn't certain how she had been nominated for this job. Sister Rachel was the one that volunteered her to help the Yoder family. But no one had consulted with her directly. Mary Ruth was annoyed about that. First, she had been sent to Leah's to help with the *kinner*. Now, she was being sent next door to help with Menno's *kinner*. All she wanted was to return home to her regular routine, not help with all of these children.

It had been two weeks since Martha Yoder's funeral. The

last place that Mary Ruth wanted to be was at the Yoder's house. It had been depressing before, even with all of those people there for the funeral. Not even busying herself in helping with the kitchen work or cleanup could erase the feeling of despair that hung in the air. Despite two weeks having passed, Mary Ruth couldn't imagine what awaited her at the house today.

While it only took fifteen minutes to walk there, it felt like an eternity. Yet, she wished it had taken even longer. Her heart pounded and her hands felt sweaty. Walking up the driveway, she noticed that the yard was overgrown and in great need of a mowing. The cows were still in the barn. No one had set them out to graze. Mary Ruth frowned. She sure hoped they had been milked. As she passed the barn, she glanced inside and noticed the milk pales by the door. They were in need of being washed but there was fresh milk on the sides. *That's gut,* she thought, as she headed toward the house.

"Hello?" she called out as she opened the door.

To her surprise, the house seemed relatively clean. Leah had told her that the church district had rotated women to help with the house and *kinner* until it was decided that Mary Ruth would step in, being next door and without her own family and home to tend. Just until Menno got back on his feet, Leah had said. Mary Ruth sure hoped that would be right quick!

"Hello?" she called out again as she set the shoofly pie on the counter.

"Who's there?" a gruff male voice called out from upstairs.

"Mary Ruth Fisher ," she replied, looking around the kitchen. It was too clean. "My sisters sent me to help today."

"Don't need no help!" The voice seemed to boom down the stairwell. There was no denying the anger and resentment in his voice. Two weeks had clearly not even begun to touch the healing process, she thought and sighed.

She sensed a movement behind her and turned, surprised to see the children staring at her from the stairwell. They wore blank expressions and dirty clothes. "Did you eat this morning?" she asked point blank.

Four heads shook from side to side.

As suspected, she thought. At least she knew what her first order of business would be. Feed the children now, deal with the angry father later. "Let me make you something to eat then," she said and hurried to the refrigerator to pull out some eggs and milk. "You can set the table while I cook."

For a moment, no one seemed to move except Mary Ruth. She pretended not to see the children, staring through the railings of the stairs at her. Instead, she went about the business of opening cabinets to look for a bowl in order to crack the eggs. She was surprised to see that each cabinet was neat and orderly. Completely different than Leah's house, she thought to herself. Despite having grown up with a mamm who secretly prided herself on having a neat and tidy house, Leah seemed to have missed acquiring that gene.

Cracking the eggs on the side of the bowl, Mary Ruth hummed to herself. It was a hymn from the Ausbund, one of her favorites. She glanced over her shoulder. The children were still staring at her. With a short little sigh, she turned back to the eggs and began to sing softly.

With pleasure and joy I will sing praises to God,
Unto the Father good,
My Spirit does strive thereafter.
For He my heart does gladden,
And with His grace stands by me always

O Lord God, You have chosen me through grade
On this earth,

And numbered me among Your children.
Therefore Your name is praised,
All my life I give thanks to You.[1]

When she stopped singing, she glanced again over her shoulder and was pleased to see Melvin walking toward her. "Would you like to stir these while I see about toasting some bread?" she asked. He nodded and took the fork from her hand, eyeing her cautiously as he reached for the bowl. "Just flick your wrist a bit," she instructed him gently and mimicked the motion with her own hand. He stared at her then did what she had told him, his eyes still on hers as if seeking reassurance that he was doing it properly. "Perfect!" she exclaimed with a smile.

Mary Ruth glanced around the kitchen, her hands on her narrow hips. "Now, where did you Mamm keep the bread?" she said softly but loud enough so that the girls could hear. "I do wonder!"

She heard the soft patter of bare feet on the floor and glanced down to see one of the girl by her side. Mary Ruth was fairly certain that her name was Suzanna. With big blue eyes and light brown hair, she was a pretty girl. Mary Ruth suspected she was about eight years old. The little girl walked over to a large drawer and pointed to it. "She keeps it there," she whispered.

"Well!" Mary Ruth said. "That's quite clever! A big drawer for the bread. Your mamm was right smart, wasn't she?"

The little girl nodded.

"Why don't you get the bread out for me and I'll get the butter. Then we need to see about setting that table. Mayhaps you could help, ja?"

The other two little girls slid down the remaining stairs and

---

[1] Ausbund Song 97 verse 1-2.

padded across the floor to help. Progress, Mary Ruth thought with just a touch of pride. While they weren't speaking, at least they were moving around and helping. That would be the beginning of healing, she told herself. And once they healed, she could go back to her regular routine.

"What is going on down here?"

She had just sat down at the table with the *kinner*, having placed a bowl of scrambled eggs in the middle, next to the cut fruit and warm toast. It wasn't much of a meal but not too shabby for last minute cooking. But the voice that shouted at her from the stairs startled her. Jumping, she almost knocked her fork onto the floor. The children stiffened and stared at the floor.

Menno Yoder stomped down the stairs and approached the table, a scowl on his face. "I asked you a question!"

Patience, she told herself. *He's hurting.* "I made some food for your *kinner*, Menno. They need to eat, ja?" She hesitated, feeling uncomfortable under his hot, angry stare. "I imagine you are hungry, too." From the looks of it, he had lost quite a bit of weight over the past two weeks since the funeral. He needed to put on more weight and regain his strength if he was going to manage this farm properly and take care of these *kinner*. "Please join us," she added.

"I don't need no invitation to eat at my own table!" he snapped. He looked at the four children and cast a glare in Mary Ruth's direction. Then, without another word, he stormed to the door, slamming his open hand against the screen door, which swung open. He disappeared outside, leaving a heavy sense of quiet in the room.

Her heart was pounding and she felt close to tears. She didn't like Menno Yoder, grief or no grief. He was rude and mean, making her forced time helping with the *kinner* seeming like a punishment, not a gesture of Christian goodwill. But she knew she had to remain strong for the children. The sooner they were self-sufficient, the sooner she wouldn't have to help and be near that Menno Yoder. "Let's pray before we eat, shall we?" she said and bowed her head for the silent prayer before their meal.

"Steve! Where are you?"

Steve looked up from the cow that he was milking. His cheek had been pressed against her warm flank as he washed her teats before the milking. It had taken him a minute to realize that someone was calling him. He was in what he called his *milking zone*, a peaceful place when he reflected and thought about all of God's blessings. When he heard his name again, he looked up and called out, "Over here!"

His younger brother, Isaac, shouted, "Phone call for you!"

With a big sigh, Steve pushed back from the cow. Before he walked away, he patted her rump gently. She didn't seem to notice or pay him any attention as she stood there, chewing some hay, waiting patiently for the release of milk from her swollen udders. "Be right back, girl," he said softly and walked out of the dairy.

Located in an old wooden shanty by the road, the phone was shared by the three families: his daed's house, his brother's house, and the tenants that lived across the street in his own farm. He wondered who would be calling him. He wasn't expecting any calls, that was for sure and certain. Curious, he picked up the pace and hurried over to the shanty. Isaac was standing nearby with a weed whacker in his hands. He had been mowing the tall grass by the road.

"Who is it?" Steve asked.

Isaac shrugged his shoulder. "Don't know." Setting the weed whacker aside, he wandered down the side of the property. He'd finish the mowing later, when Steve was no longer on the phone.

It was hot inside the phone shanty. He kept the door open for some fresh air by propping his foot against it. The phone was on a narrow shelf, the receiver resting on a stool that was in the corner. He reached for the receiver and pressed it to his ear. "Steve Fisher here."

"Steve," a female voice said. "It's Mimi Hostetler from the store."

For a moment, he frowned, trying to place the name. Mimi Hostetler. Store. Then he remembered. Mimi, the young woman who had taken his order for the replacement glass for his windows in the barn. Mimi with the big eyes and fair skin who had walked past him at the Yoder funeral. "Ja," he finally said. "I remember you."

She seemed to hesitate. "I…well…I'm calling because…" There was a long pause.

"You there?" he asked, wondering if the call had been disconnected.

"Oh ja, ja," she said. Then, taking a deep breath, she continued. "Well, your glass is in if you'd like to pick it up."

Now he was even more confused. She had told him that they would drop the glass off when Isaac's shipment of farm supplies that he had ordered. He wasn't in a hurry for the glass so there was no need to pick it up and certainly no need for her to call him. "I see," he said, although he didn't.

"Well, ja…" she stammered. "I know that I…I had said that we'd drop them off with your brother's shipment, but well…" Pause. "Well, I thought you might want to come into the store to pick it up yourself so that you could…" Pause again. "I thought maybe you wanted to fix that window sooner rather than waiting so coming into the store might be better."

She sounded nervous but Steve couldn't imagine why. It was just glass. "Uh huh," he mumbled, still trying to figure out what she was really trying to say. "I reckon I could do that."

"I mean," she continued. "It's only a short buggy ride, after all."

He shuffled his feet, the receiver feeling odd against his ear. He couldn't remember ever talking to a woman on the phone before now. It felt odd to be having a conversation with a woman he didn't know when she wasn't standing in front of him. "I don't have a buggy," he heard himself admitting.

"You what?" She sounded shocked. "How do you get around?"

"Driver."

"A driver?"

"That's what I said," he replied.

"You use a driver to go everywhere?, but how do you..." She stopped mid-sentence.

He smiled to himself. "How do I what, Mimi Hostetler?"

"Well...what I was going to say is..."

"Yes?" he prodded gently.

A short hesitation and then she blurted out, "How do you court anyone without a buggy?" Again, there was a hesitation. "Oh," she whispered. "I'm...I'm so sorry for saying that."

He found himself playing with the phone cord as he leaned against the open door and stared across the road to his farm. He had always intended to live on that farm, raise his own family. But time had passed by without any serious courting. He had liked several girls but none enough to ask for their hand in marriage. Then, as he got older, he hadn't given it much more thought. He just figured that he'd be an old *leddich* for the rest of his life, but he thought as he wrapped the curly cord around his finger, perhaps there was something in store for him after all.

"I reckon I'll be down tomorrow to pick up that glass,

Mimi," he said, smiling to himself again. "Say noon time, ja?"

As he hung up the phone, he found himself remembering her face and hearing the nervous tone in her voice just now. For the rest of the afternoon, he thought of nothing else except Mimi Hostetler and the strange phone call with the odd question. Indeed, he thought, how would I court anyone without a buggy?

The driver pulled in the next day at quarter to twelve. Steve was waiting outside, watching Katie run around in a circle, riding a long stick. He had laughed, watching as she pretended to ride her imaginary horse. When he saw the car pull into the driveway, he pushed away from the porch and walked down the stone walkway. "Better park that horse while he's pulling out, ja?" he teased Katie as he passed her.

"Whoa horsey!" she said, pulling back on the stick. She looked at her uncle and frowned. "Where you going?" It was unusual for Steve to leave the farm at mid-day. After all, the family usually shared dinner together.

"Couple of errands in town," he said and walked away.

It took almost twenty minutes to get to the store, not because it was far from the farm but because of traffic. The traffic on the main roads was terrible with almost bumper-to-bumper traffic. The driver shook his head as they crawled along Route 340. "Gets worse every year," he mumbled.

"Sure does," Steve acknowledged. He glanced at the clock. It was five minutes after twelve. He hadn't wanted to be late to pick up the glass. He had said noon and wanted Mimi Hostetler to know that he stuck by his word. "Can't change what you can't change," he added. And that sure was the truth!

There were two buggies tied up at the hitching post and one truck parked in front of the store. The driver pulled into the parking lot and shifted the gear into park. "Take as long as you need," he said as he reached for the newspaper that was on the console between them. Steve had already warned him that he wasn't certain how long it would take.

He opened the car door and stepped out. Quickly, he made certain that his shirt was tucked in and his hat on straight. He had already brushed the dirt from his boots and made certain that there were no holes in his pants. He didn't want to look unkempt and disheveled today, that was for sure and certain.

The bell over the door tingled, announcing a new customer had entered the store. Steve shut the door and let his eyes adjust to the dim light in the store. The aisles were narrow and he had to turn his body to pass a large man wearing jeans and a grey T-shirt who was bent over to look at items on a lower shelf. In the back, he saw that there were three Amish men standing by the counter. They blocked his view of the cashier.

Quietly, he headed toward the back of the store, his heart pounded and his palm sweaty. He hoped that he hadn't been wrong. He had tossed and turned all night, replaying the telephone conversation in his mind. Her voice haunted him, so sweet and innocent yet so vivacious and lively. In the morning, he had tried to milk the same cow twice and his brother had laughed at him, asking if he was in need of some coffee. Yes, he had been distracted but it wasn't coffee that he needed.

When he arrived at the back of the story, he glanced over the shoulders of the three Amish men. To his surprise and disappointment, he saw Jonas Hostetler servicing the men. Quickly and with as much discretion as he could muster, he looked around the store. There was no sign of Mimi Hostetler. She wasn't there.

He felt his heart flop inside of his chest. How could he have misread the conversation so much? He suspected that he had imagined the interest and curiosity in her voice. Perhaps, he thought, I'm lonelier than I thought. He had never been much interested in women, at least not the women that had been at the youth groups. They had silly chatter or were too interested in getting married right away. He could tell even from the first buggy ride when that was on the girl's mind, but the disappointment in his chest told him that it was time to start thinking about being alone for the rest of his life. Did he really want that?

"Steve Fisher , ja?"

He looked up and smiled at Jonas. "*Gut* to see you, Jonas."

Jonas nodded, his eyes twinkling as he tugged at his beard. "Sorry to hear about your windows. Terrible thing, ain't so? These Englischer boys need more things to occupy their time."

Steve nodded, his eyes once again flickering around the back of the store. "I agree, ja."

"So, if I recall, you came to pick up that glass," Jonas said, shuffling through some papers. "We could have dropped them off for you," he added. "But I understand being in a hurry to fix the barn windows."

Steve frowned and looked at Jonas. He was about to say something, to mention that his daughter had called him to pick up the glass, when there was a burst of life in the back of the store. The back door opened and Mimi hurried into the store. "Daed," she said, breathlessly. "Mamm says to come for dinner. I'll take over this customer." She lifted her eyes to look at Steve then quickly looked away.

He tried to hide his smile. He hadn't imagined it after all.

"Ja? But what about you? You need some dinner, *Dochder*."

Mimi shrugged. "Mamm will save me a plate." She chewed on her lower lip and motioned toward the door. "She said to hurry or else it would get cold."

Jonas shook his head as he stepped away from the counter, making room for Mimi to take his place. He looked at Steve and laughed. "You know how these woman fuss about their food," he teased.

"My mamm is the same, I reckon," he offered meekly. He didn't want to admit that, no, he didn't know about women fussing.

For a moment, there was silence. Jonas left the store and Steve stood awkwardly at the counter. Mimi shuffled through the same papers that her daed had been looking through. The noise sounded loud in the silence of the store.

"Let's see," she said, her head bent over the papers. "I believe you came in for some window glass, ja?"

"I believe so," he replied, trying to hide his smile again. She was charming, he thought, trying to behave as if she hadn't called him yesterday.

The man in the jeans and T-shirt walked over to the counter, carrying an armload of tools. He stood behind Steve, waiting for his turn.

Mimi looked up and saw the man. Her face paled and she looked over at Steve. "Since I'll have to find your order, would you mind…?" She didn't finish her statement.

He nodded and stepped aside, glad that he wasn't going to be rushed. It was worth the wait. Besides, while she was busy helping the other customer, he was able to watch her without feeling too conspicuous.

Her voice was soft and kind as she greeted the other man. She looked him in the eyes when he spoke and smiled when she took the items from him to ring up on the cash register. There was something gentle yet strong about her. She was different than any other woman he had met. Usually they were shy and quiet around men, especially Englischers. The unmarried women he knew also tended to look away from men, too bashful to hold a steady gaze for long. Yes, Mimi Hostetler was different, indeed.

By the time that the man left, Steve had a new pounding

inside of his chest. It had been years since he had thought about a woman and now, with Mimi standing before him, he was determined that today would change his future.

"Now," she said, smiling and feeling more confident. "Let's see if we can find that glass, shall we?"

"Do you need help?" he offered.

For a moment, she hesitated. Once again, he wondered if he had been wrong. Had he misread everything? Why didn't she respond? But he kept her gaze and waited patiently for her to mull over his question. Finally, she nodded. "That would be right gut, Steve Fisher . Normally we don't let customers into the storeroom but I sure would hate to break that heavy glass."

He doubted that she couldn't carry the glass herself but appreciated the humility of her response. Walking around the counter, he followed her into the back room. She was shorter than he was, almost by six inches. And her frame was narrow and petite. Yet, there was something about her that spoke of both physical and spiritual strength.

"I do believe the glass is back here," she said, pointing toward a corner. "Behind those boxes."

He moved past her, his arm brushing against hers, as he moved in the direction that she indicated. He felt tingles throughout his body and glanced at her, ready to apologize but speechless when he saw her cheeks flush pink. She gave him a small smile then took a step back.

Carefully, he moved the boxes and stacked them in the walkway. Only then did he see the wrapped pieces of glass leaning against he wall. He felt it was strange that they would be tucked so far away, especially since he had told her that he would pick them up today. But then again, he realized, maybe she had not dug them out of the storeroom on purpose.

He lifted the two flat packages and carried them out to the

counter. She walked behind him. When he turned around to go back to the storeroom in order to put the boxes back, he bumped into her.

"I'm sorry," he said, reaching his hands out to steady her. When he touched her arms, she looked up at him and met his gaze. He swallowed, feeling completely thunderstruck by her expression, so young and innocent yet full of hope. "You all right?"

She nodded, another pink crimson covering her cheeks. "Ja, of course."

He hurried back into the storeroom and returned the boxes to their proper place. She was leaning against the door, watching him. He could feel her eyes on his back. Her attention made him more aware of his actions and he worked faster.

"There!" he said, standing up and rubbing his hands together to wipe away the dust. He looked over at her and smiled. "Right as rain."

"*Danke*, Steve Fisher ," she said softly.

Taking a deep breath, he headed back toward the front of the store, pausing to let her step back as he passed her. *Now*, he thought. *Ask her now.* "I was thinking…" he began as he repositioned himself by the front of the counter while she began to ring up the sale.

"Ja?"

He noticed that she didn't look up that time. She was busy writing on the paper and using the calculator to figure out taxes on the order. "*Ach vell*," he continued, pulling his hat off of his head and running this fingers through his curly hair. "You see, I might not have a buggy, Mimi Hostetler," he said, feeling awkward. Shuffling on his feet, he held his hat in front of him. "But mayhaps you might like to go for a walk some evening?"

She looked up, her eyes wide and surprised. "A walk?"

He cleared his throat, feeling uncomfortable under her

gaze. *What does that look mean,* he wondered. "Or…well… mayhaps a picnic by a pond."

She set the pencil down, never once removing her eyes from his face. "How would I get there?"

He blinked. He hadn't expected that question. "I…well…"

"In a car?" she asked, frowning. Apparently that idea didn't sit well with her.

"*Nee,*" he said quickly. *A buggy, a buggy, where to get a buggy?* His mind rattled over the possibilities and quickly he said, "I reckon I could borrow a buggy and pick you up." He rubbed at the back of his neck. "My daed and my brother have one that I could borrow, I'm sure."

Tapping the pencil against the paper, she kept staring at him but didn't respond. He watched as she chewed on her lower lip for a second. Then, she bent her head back down to return to writing something on the paper. "I suppose that would be right nice," she said and ripped the paper from a pad of paper. Smiling, she handed it to him. "That would be right nice, indeed."

He took the paper. "What is this?"

"Your invoice. The police said you should give it to them and they will pay for the replacement glass," she explained. "I'm off on Mondays and Tuesdays," she added.

"Mondays and Tuesdays?"

"For our picnic," she said.

"Oh!" He felt foolish. It had been years since he had asked a young woman to ride in a buggy with him. Ten years at least, he thought. He was so stunned that he had done it, had asked this charming young woman on a picnic and, what's more, she had said yes. "Of course. Monday then."

He carried his glass out of the store, his head still whirling. He wasn't certain how all of this had happened but he knew one thing was for certain. If he intended to court Mimi Hostetler, he would have to make another acquisition quite soon. After all, what was a courting man without a horse and buggy to spend private moments alone with his intended?

The driver was waiting for him and, when he saw Steve walking out to the car, he quickly opened his door and hurried to the trunk. They laid the glass down and he covered it with a soft, faded quilt. "Get everything you need, then?" the driver asked.

"Oh ja," Steve replied. Monday sure seemed far away. It was only Thursday and there was no church this upcoming week. Four days until the picnic with Mimi Hostetler. Four days to think about her sparkling eyes and crimson cheeks. "I sure did get everything I need, indeed." And he smiled as he looked out the window while the driver backed out of the driveway to take him back to his farm.

Katie saw her uncle lift the large, flat packages from the back of the car. He leaned them against the barn and paid the driver. She had been playing outside with Ben and the other *kinner*. They laughed and tossed a ball back and forth, trying to tease the dog, Shep, into stealing it from them. As the car had pulled into the driveway, however, everyone had lost interest in the game, including the dog.

"What's you got there?" Ben asked, his hands thrust into his pockets as he stood on his dirty tippy toes, trying to see. "Looks big!"

"Sure is," Steve said, feeling more jovial and happy than he had in years. "Glass for the broken windows to my barn."

"Oh!" Ben gasped. "From the bad men."

He laughed. "Well, what they did is bad but mayhaps they are not bad through and through."

The little boy frowned. "Not so certain about that," he

mumbled and, losing interest, he ran back to the other *kinner* to return to their game.

Katie had watched from afar, surprised to see her *onkel* Steve so happy and laughing. He was usually so quiet and withdrawn. Frowning, she walked into the kitchen to find her mamm busy in the kitchen. Her mamm seemed to always be busy in the kitchen.

"Steve got his glass for the windows," she announced, sliding onto the bench by the table. They had just finished eating dinner and her mamm was busy cleaning up the dishes. "Thought he said that they were going to drop them off," she said. "Wonder why he went to pick them up, then?"

"Well," Anna said as she started stacking dishes to put them away in the cabinet. "He must have wanted to get that new glass put in early."

"Why, you think?"

The questions. Always the questions, Anna thought as she sighed and shut the cabinet door. "Why what?"

"Why would he want to do that? He had to hire a driver to go pick them up. Seems like a waste of money and time," Katie said, making a face. "Ain't so?"

Her mamm turned around and put her hand on her hip. "You are very *balaadsche*! It gets tiresome, all those questions while I'm working, Katie." Anna frowned at her daughter, angry with herself for being so irritated. She tried to soften her tone. "Besides, I think you might have some chores to do, anyway. That garden could sure use some time spent weeding. Go get your *bruder* to help."

"Aw," Katie whined. "Weeding?"

"I don't appreciate that tone," Anna said softly, still trying to maintain her temper but leveling her gaze to stare directly at her daughter. "Now you get outside and take a bucket to weed. I'll be out in an hour to see how you are coming along." She paused. "If you do a good job, we can make a shoo-fly pie this afternoon for after supper."

Katie slid around on the bench and stood up. "Bet it won't be as good as Leah's!" she mumbled.

"Scoot!"

Katie could tell that her mamm was frustrated. She wasn't certain why she always sounded so impatient with her. She had questions, that's all. Questions that just begged to be asked. The only problem was that no one ever wanted to answer them.

She wandered over to the garden and stared at the tall weeds that peered back. She hated weeding. The feel of the dirt under her nails bothered her. It dried out her feet and hands, too. No amount of soap ever seemed to rid her skin from the dry, dusty feeling. And it smelled funny, too. No, she didn't like dirt and gardens at all. She much preferred helping her mamm in the house or daed in the barn.

So when she heard the car engine pulling down the driveway, she was quick to jump up and run out of the garden toward the noise. She peered around the side of the garden shed to see who was driving up toward the house. Any visitor would mean a break from working in the hot sun and dry, smelly garden.

Eleanor, she thought with a big grin. The car was the same one as last time. Katie would recognize it anywhere. And when the door swung open, she could barely contain her excitement to see a pair of cowboy boots step onto the driveway. Katie wanted to run over toward her but held herself back. Instead, she slipped behind the shed and ran to the porch.

"Mamm!"

Her mother turned around and put a hand on her hip. "I thought I told you to weed the garden!"

"But Mamm!" she said between gasps for air. "Eleanor is

back!"

Anna started to say something but stopped before any words came out. Instead, she glanced around the kitchen, seeing that, despite her best efforts, everything was a mess.

Chapter 4: Anna's Letter

Dear Family,

It was wunderbaar to receive the package of letters from Rachel and Leah so soon after Mamm started the circle letter. I can hardly wait until the package returns at the end of the circle with the second round of letters!

As usual, we are busy at the farm. The kinner are enjoying the gut weather for playing and the men are thankful for no rain during hay cutting time. They were able to cut and bale during the same week, which was a blessing from the good Lord, indeed.

We sure do miss having Mary Ruth here but are ever so grateful that she has been able to help those poor kinner of Martha Yoder. We sure thought and prayed for the Yoder family, especially during our own baling work.

Steve has been busy helping Isaac as well as working next door at his own farm. We hardly see him anymore. I do know that he's been borrowing Isaac's buggy from time to time. Must be having problems getting his driver for shorter distances.

Mamm and Daed are doing well. Mamm and I went to market the other day to buy beets for canning since our crop didn't turn so well. We were surprised to find the kinner's dog, Shep, asleep in the back when we moved the seat to put our box of goods. We had quite a laugh over that one. He's been taking to sleeping in the buggy at night anyhow.

Our friend Eleanor stopped by the other day and has made an offer to let Katie ride one of her ponies that will be boarded at Gideon Riehl's farm, over near sister Rachel and Leah. I reckon that will mean some more frequent visits, which will be right gut. Of course, Isaac hasn't made up his mind yet if he will agree to such an arrangement.

Looking forward to Church Sunday at Leah's next week. It will be a glorious day to share fellowship with the entire family...or at least those that can attend.

Blessings and love to all of you.

Anna and family

"Something's going on with *bruder* Steve," Isaac said as he washed his hands in the sink before the dinner meal. He had just walked into the kitchen and, after smiling at Anna, had walked over to the bench to remove his boots before cleaning up. He didn't seem to notice the cluttered counters and the toys scattered across the dirty floor. Under the table, a spoon from the morning meal lay next to a torn piece of newspaper. But he was oblivious to the mess.

"How so?" Anna asked, hurrying to start putting the food on the table.

"Twice in one week that he asked to borrow Tripper to go to town."

Anna stopped moving, motionless as she held a bowl of steaming boiled potatoes. She stared at her husband, her mouth hanging open in a delicate O shape. "The horse and buggy?"

"Ja," Isaac said, smiling.

"The horse and buggy?" she repeated, as if she didn't believe that her husband had heard her properly.

He laughed. "The horse and buggy," he repeated.

Anna's mouth fell open. "You don't say!"

He tried not to laugh. "I believe I did say," he teased.

Setting the bowl of potatoes on the table, she sat down next to her husband. "You don't think that…" but she couldn't complete the sentence. The door opened and the children began to romp into the kitchen. Such talk with adult questions was not to be shared with the *kinner*. But Anna knew that she was not likely to forget her questions for later. She certainly wanted to know more about Steve and this horse and buggy business! He hadn't driven a horse and buggy for years, opting to use a driver for his errands which were far and few between.

After a silent blessing, all of their heads bowed and hands pressed together on their laps, the routine chaos of mealtime commenced. Bowls of steaming hot vegetables were passed around and no one was shy. Potatoes, corn on the cob, chilled applesauce, warm red beets, and fresh bread were hoarded onto the plates. No one complained about the food, not even the smallest child. When the beef and gravy was passed, the children stared at the bowl, their eyes wide and bright, eager for their mamm's good cooking. But each waited their turn as the bowl was passed from daed to mamm then around the table.

"Gonna be cutting hay again tomorrow. With all the *gut* rain and sunshine, the good Lord is blessing us with another crop," Isaac, said, the corn in his hands before his mouth. When he finished talking, he began to eat it. Then after a minute, he added: "Be needing you *kinner* to help."

Katie looked up, her eyes sparkling. She always loved working outdoors, much more than inside housework. And when Isaac had fieldwork that required the help of all capable children, Katie was always the first one to eagerly volunteer. "That means me, Daed?"

He smiled. "Sure does, Katie. Many hands…" he started.

The *kinner* joined in as a chorus: "…make light the work." They broke into peels of laughter and Isaac smiled at their silliness.

Anna handed the bowl of applesauce to Benjamin and motioned for him to pass it down the row. "Isaac, with Katie being so big and helpful, sure does seem like she's much more responsible these days, ain't so?" She looked up and, when Katie stared at her, she smiled at her daughter. "Mayhaps you have something you want to be telling her, husband?"

For a moment, Isaac took a deep breath and ignored Katie's anxious gaze. He seemed to be drawing it out as he continued to eat the rows of kernels on his corncob. Then, setting it down on his plate, he wiped his hands and mouth on his napkin. "Well, Anna, reckon you mayhaps have a point there." He turned to stare at his youngest daughter. "Your mamm and I have been talking about this arrangement with Eleanor Haile," he started.

Katie sat up straight and stared at him. Her face seemed to lose its color as she waited for his proclamation. It was the moment she had been waiting for, quietly in the shadows. She had been too afraid to ask, for fear of angering her daed at her impatience. When no one had mentioned it for almost a week, she had all but given up on any hope of riding those ponies.

"We think we will let you go over to Gideon Riehl's with Eleanor Haile," he said slowly. She gasped out loud and the other *kinner* began to clamor about, their eyes bright and sparkling. Before there was too much commotion, Isaac silenced them by holding up his hand. "Wait, Katie, there's more."

Quiet fell over the table.

"If you learn how to ride that pony and care for it under Eleanor's instruction," he said then paused, sneaking a glance at Anna before he continued. "We'll let you bring that pony to the farm."

"Here?" she squeaked.

"Ja, here," Anna added softly.

Isaac held up his hand again when he saw that Katie was about to leap from her seat and hug her mamm. "But only if you pass muster with Eleanor. You know naught about pony care and I don't have time to tend its needs. I need to know that you can care for it without my time being taken over."

"Oh Daed!" she gushed. "I won't bother you one bit."

He made a face, glancing at Anna again and trying to hide his pleasure with his daughter's excitement. "We'll just see about that now, won't we?", but as she leapt from her bench and threw her arms around his neck, even Anna noticed the hint of tears at the corner of his eyes. It was a rare moment when a parent could do something as special as what Isaac had just agreed to do for Katie. She was pleased that her daughter appreciated it and prayed that Katie would rise to the occasion in tending the pony's needs.

"Enough talk about ponies," Anna said with a smile. She didn't want the other *kinner* thinking that Katie was getting special treatment or being singled out. "I have a surprise for dessert today! I made apple crunch." The younger children clapped their hands in delight and even Isaac looked up, beaming. "But no one gets any pie until those plates are cleaned off of your dinner," she added, smiling back at her family.

Mary Ruth counted to ten for the third time in less than thirty minutes. She had her back to the room and her hands were on the counter, pressing hard against the cool linoleum top. Her eyes were scrunched shut and she tried to calm her heart when, in truth, she wished she could turn around and give that Menno Yoder the what-for that was begging to jump from her lips.

"Don't want you here! I done told you that every day that you been here!" He was shouting at her, pushing the kitchen chairs aside and knocking plates to the floor. The noise was loud and Mary Ruth had to fight extra hard to not jump. She had never before seen anyone rage like that.

The *kinner* were standing in the mudroom, clinging to each other as they watched their daed rant and rave as he had every day for the past two weeks. This time, however, he was throwing things and shouting louder than ever.

"You keep moving things around! Those pans!" He pointed at the wall where the pots and pans hung, moving closer to them. He knocked one off the wall and it clattered to the ground. "Martha don't keep them up there like that!" He hurried over to a drawer and yanked it open. "And this? What's this?"

Mary Ruth glanced over her shoulder, her eyes narrow and cool. "That is called a drawer."

He glared at her. "Don't sass me! I know it's a drawer. But what did you do with it?"

Mary Ruth exhaled sharply. He was trying her patience, that was for sure and certain. "I organized it. It was a jumble of things and there was no way to find anything."

"That's not the way she left it!" he shouted, his voice booming through the house.

"No," she said slowly, turning around. She put her hands on his hips as she faced him. "No Menno, it's not how Martha left it. But Martha is no longer here and you have to start accepting the help of the community, the people who care about you."

He stopped in mid-step and glared at her. "I don't want their help and don't want them caring about me."

Reaching for the dishtowel, she dried her hand on it. She was acting calmer than she felt. She wasn't certain where that strength was coming from, truth be told. His behavior scared her. "Well, you keep behaving this way and that will be sure and certain to happen!" Her words came out sharper than she intended but she masked her own surprise.

For a moment, she saw a glimmer. She wasn't certain what it meant but she saw him pause and take a deep breath.

"Look Menno," Mary Ruth said, trying to soften her tone. "You have four *kinner* that need you and your tirades against me sure aren't helping them." She glanced at them and, for the briefest moment, her eyes caught Melvin's. Her heart swelled at the sight of him. *My special project,* she thought.

"I didn't invite you," he stated firmly but without the previous anger in his tone.

"No," she agreed. "No, you surely didn't. And you have make it quite clear how much I am welcomed here."

"Then go!"

She shook her head, forcing herself to show a strength that she didn't necessarily feel. "And face the wrath of my sister, Rachel? *Danke,* but no," she said. "Besides, your children need me. Who will feed them? Who will clean up this kitchen? Wash their clothing?" She saw him tense and tried to calm him down by lowering her voice. "Your *g'may* cares about you and your *kinner,* Menno Yoder. Let us help you." She paused before she added, "Don't you think it's what Martha would have wanted? If not for you, then for her *kinner*?"

There was a long pause. Neither Menno nor Mary Ruth spoke. She stared at him, wondering if she had pushed him just too far this time. His face seemed to tense up and the color drained from it. She saw him clench his jaw as he pressed his lips together, tight and angry. But he said nothing.

For the past two weeks, she had been fulfilling her duty and walking to the Yoder farm every day in order to get the children fed, the house cleaned, the laundry washed, and the kitchen organized. Each day, she had been confronted with angry glares from Menno who, on most mornings, stormed out of the house and never returned. That had been fine with Mary Ruth. The children had begun to open up to her and, despite her own reluctance to allow them close to her heart, she found herself becoming fond of them in a way she had never known possible.

The two older girls were clingy, afraid to let Mary Ruth out of their sight while the younger girl was more of the shy sort. She would watch her from a distance, a thumb stuck into her mouth. Mary Ruth ignored her curious gaze and silence by continuing to include her in the discussion, even if she didn't reply. But it was Melvin who caused her the most angst. He often disappeared and, when Mary Ruth would look for him, she'd find him sitting somewhere alone, staring at the wall. He showed little to no interest in anything but he was never disrespectful. Mary Ruth would reach for his hand and help him to his feet, leading him back into the kitchen and assigning him a task to keep him busy and within her eyesight.

The previous evening, his behavior bothered her so much that Mary Ruth wandered over to Rachel's to ask for advice. To her surprise, Elijah was downstairs, sleeping in a chair. Placing a finger on her lips, Rachel motioned that they should move into the other room so as not to disturb him.

"He's still fighting that cold," Rachel explained in a hushed whisper. "I thought he was over it but it came back." She wore a concerned look on her face. "I want him to sleep as much as he can. That cough just keeps him up all night."

"I'm sorry to hear that," Mary Ruth said and she meant it. The past two weeks had provided Mary Ruth with a new perspective on life and relationships. "I won't stay long, sister, but I need your advice about Melvin Yoder. He's still so reclusive and sad."

Rachel frowned. "Of course he is! He lost his mamm!"

"I understand that," Mary Ruth quickly replied. "But I don't know what to do to help him." When she heard Elijah cough, she lowered her voice. "Given that you volunteered me to help them through this rough patch, mayhaps you can guide me a bit, ja?"

Her eldest sister sighed and shook her head. Clearly this was new territory for her, too. "I just don't know, Mary Ruth. Being there, being consistent, and being kind but firm…that's what children need," she offered. "Keep doing what you are doing and try to get that Menno to see past his grief." They both heard Elijah cough again. This time, he had gotten up from his chair and shuffled up the stairs. "I need to go check on him. Get him some tea to soothe his throat and help him sleep," Rachel said. "I'll pray on your situation, Mary Ruth."

Now, as Mary Ruth stood in the kitchen, facing Menno Yoder, she wondered if he would ever get past his grief so that she could return home.

"I'm making a nice dinner today for your *kinner*," Mary Ruth said, breaking the silence. "Mayhaps it would be nice if you joined them. It has been three weeks, Menno, and I know that seems fresh in your mind. But your mourning the dead doesn't help those who are living." She held his angry gaze as she gently added, "They need you."

Without a word, he turned around and stormed out of the kitchen. When the door slammed shut, the *kinner* stared at her, their eyes wide and frightened. Mary Ruth leaned against the counter and tried to still her pounding heart. She was angry. Angry at Rachel for having volunteered her for this horrible task. Angry at Menno for ignoring those children. And angry with herself for not being stronger in standing up to him.

Shutting her eyes, she repeated her favorite Proverbs verse for when she was upset: *Trust in the Lord with all your heart and lean not onto thy own understanding - in all the ways acknowledge*

Him and He will direct your paths.[2] A wave of guilt fled through her as she realized that, by being angry, she was doubting the Lord and His infinite wisdom. After all, she reminded herself, He is our Father and He cares for His children. If only she knew what path He was directing her toward.

"Let's get to our chores, shall we?" she said, breaking the silence and forcing a smile.

Anna looked up when Steve walked into the kitchen. He wasn't wearing his typical work clothes. Rather, he had on a clean shirt and pants. She noticed that he even wore his nice boots, not the ones that he typically wore in the barnyard.

"Heading out. Isaac said you have some plates to take over to Rachel and Leah?"

Anna peered at him, studying his face for a quick moment. There was something about him, a glow. "Ja, I heard you were riding over that direction." She paused. She wasn't certain how much she could push her brother-in-law. "Borrowing the buggy again, ain't so?"

He mumbled something under his breath.

"I didn't hear you," she said.

"Ja, the buggy. Nice weather for a ride. Need some time to think, I reckon," he said.

"Um hum," Anna commented, a hand on her hip. "Something is up with you, Steve Fisher !"

"The apple crunch pie? Where is it?"

"You are avoiding the question."

"You didn't ask no question," he scoffed. Clearly, he didn't

---

[2] Proverbs 3:5,6

want to talk. "If you want me delivering them, you best hurry along, sister."

Hiding a smile, Anna hurried into the back room where she had put the apple crunch pies into large plastic containers for protection on the journey. She glanced through the open door at Steve, watching as he drummed his fingers on the counter and tapped his foot. He was impatient and anxious. Something is up with him, indeed, she told herself.

"Don't forget to return the containers, Steve," Anna said as she started to hand them over to him. "Will be needing them for church Sunday at Leah's."

"Ja, ja," he said gruffly.

"You sure do look nice for just taking a buggy ride to think," Anna added, watching his face for a reaction. It was true. He was dressed in clean black pants and a fresh white shirt. Normally, Steve wore his regular work clothes all day and saved the good clothing for church Sunday. She couldn't remember the last time he had changed during the week.

Steve frowned at her, took the containers, and walked out of the kitchen without another word. She turned to watch him from the kitchen window but he disappeared quickly around the side of the barn. A few minutes later, she heard the familiar rattle of the buggy wheels as the horse pulled out of the driveway and down the road.

Anna hurried over to Miriam's side of the house. She found her mother-in-law crocheting in her favorite chair by the window. The sun was high and bright, shining into the room and basking everything in a lovely summer glow.

"Mamm!" Anna said, sitting down on the sofa next to her. "Steve borrowed the buggy again."

Miriam looked up, her fingers still moving as she continued making her placemat. "Did he, now?"

"You don't think…?"

Miriam laughed. "Oh Anna," she set her work down on her lap. "At his age?" She smiled at her daughter-in-law. They had always had a good relationship. Anna was different than her own daughters, much more open and friendly, eager to be a part of the family from day one. In fact, Miriam often felt closer to her than her own natural daughters. It was just like Anna to hope that Steve was interested in someone. "You do have the most fanciful ideas," she said gently. She certainly didn't want to hurt Anna's feelings. "But I think his time has come and gone. Where would he meet someone anyway? It's not as if he goes running around with the younger ones and he works from before sunrise to well after sunset."

Slumping onto the sofa, Anna sighed. She was so hopeful that Steve would find someone to share his life with. He was such a kind man who honored God in every aspect of his daily life. It was a shame to not share it with another godly woman. "I reckon you're right," she conceded. "Of course, I still wonder about the buggy…"

Picking up her work from her lap, Miriam returned to crocheting. Anna watched her mother-in-law's fingers move, a fluid motion of wrapping the yarn around the crochet hook and pulling it through the loop in the chain. It was almost musical in nature. Her hands moved so quickly, feeding the yarn to the crochet hook as if she were a machine. It was beautiful to watch. And, while doing this, her mother-in-law was obviously involved in deep thoughts. "Mayhaps he just wants more freedom than he gets when he hires those Englische drivers."

"I suppose," Anna said. But she wasn't really convinced.

Steve pulled the buggy alongside Mary Ruth. He had spotted her on the road, walking back to Leah's house from the

Yoder's farm. He hadn't been certain that it was his sister at first but he remembered that she was helping the widower during his transition. He didn't envy his sister and said a silent prayer of gratitude to God that he had been born a man and a farmer. Women seemed to get moved around a lot before marriage, working at markets, stores, or houses while a man who farmed had a steady routine.

When he stopped the buggy, Mary Ruth looked up at him in complete surprise. "Steve! What on earth…?"

He shrugged his shoulders. "Felt like taking a ride. Plus Anna asked me to drop off these apple crunch pies." He motioned for Mary Ruth to climb into the buggy. It jiggled under her weight as she settled next to him on the blue velour seat. "How you making out over here?" he asked.

"Don't ask," she said glumly. "That Yoder man is miserable. And I feel like I'm just cleaning up after everyone, Menno's house in the morning and Leah's in the afternoon! I just want to come home."

He nodded his head as if he understood what she meant. It didn't sound like fun having to help a fresh widow pick up the pieces to his life, especially one that was known for being a bit on the stubborn side. Slapping the reins on the horse's back and clucking his tongue, Steve directed the horse down the road. The buggy lurched forward as it began to roll along.

"What's new at home anyway?" she asked, her heart heavy with longing for her own bed and Mamm's good home cooking. If Leah was a poor housekeeper, she was an even poorer cook.

"Not much," he said. Then, as if an after-thought, he added, "Isaac is going to let Katie tend to that Eleanor woman's pony at Gideon's place."

"A pony?" Mary Ruth repeated and raised an eyebrow. "What's that about?"

Steve slowed the horse down as a car sped past on his left. "That Eleanor is boarding some ponies at Gideon's farm for a while and Katie wants to care for one. Isaac and Anna think it will help calm her spirit a bit to take on that responsibility. If it works, they will keep the pony at our farm."

"Gideon's farm is just on the other side of the Yoders' place, ain't so?" The wheels in her mind were turning, an idea forming that gave her hope on how to get the Yoder family in shape so that she could finally return home.

Steve nodded. "Ja," he said. "Oh and that Shep…crazy dog! Seems to like sleeping in the buggy. Isaac keeps finding him curled up in the back. The other day, he was halfway to the market when the dog woke up and jumped onto the seat next to him. Scared Isaac half to death!"

They both laughed.

It was half an hour before he managed to escape Leah's chaotic house. It always amazed him how Leah could be so very different from his other sisters. Unorganized, frantic and more than a little self-absorbed. He just shook his head thinking about how Mary Ruth had been forced to stay there. He knew that they had she had her work cut out for her at Leah's. He wondered how her husband, Jonah, could put up with the chaos and mess in the house.

As the horse drove down the road, he began to think about Mimi. He couldn't imagine her being like Leah. No, he thought. Mimi was certainly a tidy housekeeper and hard-worker. If he had learned anything about her, he had learned that.

Today, he was picking her up for a nice long buggy ride and a stroll in the park. It would be the third time that they had spent time together. He smiled to himself, remembering their picnic last week. She had been delightful company. In fact, he couldn't remember the last time he had smiled and laughed so much. She had a funny way of looking at things and saying what she meant. And her energy! She was full of it.

When he pulled up to the Hostetler's farm, he was glad that she was already outside. He wasn't ready to have to talk to her parents or deal with the suspicions from the community. Ideal minds meant overactive tongues, his mamm had always said. For that reason, he was especially grateful that she lived in a different church district. That would help keep the questions at bay. But it sure was difficult dealing with the questions at home whenever he needed to borrow a buggy.

"Well hello there, Steve Fisher ," she said jovially as she slid open the door to the buggy and peered inside. Her eyes flashed and she smiled brightly at him. "What brings you here, today?"

For a moment, he looked confused and quickly reached into his memory. Today was the day that he had mentioned going for a buggy ride, wasn't it? "I..I thought that…"

Mimi laughed and climbed into the buggy, settling down next to him. "I'm teasing you," she said, nudging him gently with her elbow. "Did you think I forgot?"

His heart swelled. She was so very different from other girls, full of surprises and joy. He liked that very much. Other girls were not as confident and tended to be quiet and shy. He had always dreaded those types of girls and avoided them when he was younger. On the few occasions that he had taken a girl home from a singing, the rides had been quiet and subdued. It was as if the girls were afraid to open their mouths and speak.

Not Mimi Hostetler.

"Where shall we go today, then?" he asked.

Pursing her lips, she appeared deep in thought. Then, smiling, she said, "How about some ice cream? It's a nice day for it, ja?"

The horse walked slowly down the road. Steve made certain to purposefully keep some tension in the reins, willing the horse to keep the slow and steady pace. He listened to her tell him about her week at the store. She laughed about the Englischer customers who pretended to peruse the aisles when all they really wanted was to talk with an Amish person. She told him that another barn had been vandalized on the other side of town. And she mentioned that she was looking forward to church Sunday at Leah's house in the upcoming week.

"Will you be there?" she asked curiously.

"Ja, I imagine," he said. "Whole family is likely to attend. I know my mamm and sisters are planning to come up to help with the cooking and to clean the house."

Mimi nodded but didn't respond. Leah's poor housekeeping was common knowledge and Steve was appreciative that Mimi was respectful enough not to comment.

"I don't recall seeing you there before," she said casually.

"*Nee*," he admitted. "Never went before. Stuck to my own district."

"Really?" She stared up at him with large, bright eyes. "So why are you coming this year?"

He glanced at her and felt his heart jump when he saw her eyes. So sparkling and full of life. Her entire face seemed to glow and he felt himself feeling weak. For the past two weeks, he had been praying to God, asking for guidance. He didn't want to get his hopes up, hopes that someone as marvelously godly and wonderful as Mimi Hostetler might actually be interested in him, but seeing her hopeful eyes gazing at him, he knew.

"I…" He wasn't certain how to respond, but clearly she was waiting. "I guess that…"

"Ja?" she asked.

"I don't want to presume anything but…"

"Go on," she prodded gently.

He cleared his throat and took a deep breath. "I sure do like spending time in your company, Mimi Hostetler."

A hint of a smile tilted the corner of her mouth. "Is that so?"

He stared straight ahead, afraid to look at her. "And if you feel the same, well…"

"I do."

He paused. "You do what?"

"Enjoy your company, Steve Fisher."

And there it was.

His heart pounded and he caught his breath. After so many years, it had finally happened. He had given up, that was for sure and certain. He had never expected to find someone but now, here he was riding alongside a beautiful young woman who had just told him that she enjoyed his company. And that meant only one thing: *they were courting.* Officially courting.

He swallowed, a moment of panic rising in his throat. He had never before truly courted anyone. Just a few rides home from singings but never with the same girl twice. Now, it was official. He didn't know what to say or what was expected. Certainly they would keep spending time together and, if all went well, he knew that an announcement would be forthcoming. The pit in his stomach grew larger. *An announcement?*

He felt her hand on his arm. Once again, he looked at her. With her hair pulled back so neat and shiny under her prayer kapp and her face glowing, she was truly beautiful. Her goodness shone from the inside out.

"You look pale, Steve," she said softly. It was as if she could sense his nervousness. "Are you OK?"

"I…I just didn't expect any of this," he admitted. He disliked feeling flustered and, even more, he hated sounding so naïve. But it was the truth and, if nothing else, he knew that courting meant discovery and truth.

Mimi took a deep breath and reassured him with a smile that warmed his heart. "Nor did I," she replied. Yet, she looked confident and content as she settled back into the buggy seat next to him, her arm lightly pressed against his. "But God sure does work in mysterious ways, that's for sure and certain!"

Anna was washing the dinner dishes when she heard the buggy roll down the driveway. She glanced out the window then looked at the clock. Steve had been gone for over three hours and had missed helping Isaac with the milking. She hoped nothing was wrong over at Rachel and Leah's.

She could see Isaac on the hill in the back field. Despite Steve's disappearance, Isaac had finished the early evening milking and had let the cows wander back into the paddock to graze throughout the night. Now, he was walking along the fence line, checking it for breaks. Katie and Benjamin were chasing each other through the field, keeping him company. Shep was running alongside. It was the perfect moment and she smiled to herself, feeling God's love surrounding her and her family.

Shutting off the water, she reached for the dishtowel and dried her hands. She was hoping to have a moment alone with Steve, see if she could uncover where he had been all day and make certain that everything was all right at his sisters' farms.

The door opened and he walked in, carrying the two containers. He seemed far away and barely said more than hello to Anna. He set the containers on the table and walked across the kitchen floor toward the door that led to the great room, the room reserved for church Sunday, which connected both sides of the house. She stood at the counter, a hand on her hip as she watched him, her mouth hanging open.

"Steve?"

He stopped and looked up. "Ja?"

"You OK?"

He nodded and said dismissively, "Ja, ja."

Anna frowned. "You feeling poorly?"

He looked surprised. "No, not in the least."

"Everything all right at Leah and Rachel's?"

He frowned. "Of course." And then he disappeared through the doorway.

What in the world, she thought, staring at the space where he had just passed through. Determined to find out what was going on, Anna set the towel on the counter and followed him. Her younger *kinner* were visiting with Miriam so she would just go over there to collect them in preparation for bedtime, but in truth, she wanted to see if Miriam noticed Steve's strange behavior.

The *kinner* were playing with an alphabet puzzle, laying out the pieces along the floor. Miriam was back in her chair, crocheting while there was still daylight. Anna looked around. The room was empty, besides Miriam. Had she imagined that strange conversation?

"Did Steve just pass through here?" she asked, walking toward Miriam. She glanced around the room again.

Looking up at her daughter-in-law, Miriam frowned. "Ja. He said he was going to bed. Early day tomorrow."

"Mamm," Anna said, sitting down on the sofa. "He just walked through my kitchen as if he wasn't even there!"

She laughed. "Of course he was there, if he walked through the kitchen!"

Anna shook her head. How could she explain it so that Miriam would understand? "That's not what I meant. He was somewhere else, barely said hello, and just kept on walking. Something's wrong."

With a familiar tsk, tsk of her tongue and a frown, Miriam raised an eyebrow at Anna. "Best be thinking of something else, Anna. If he wants us to know what's on his mind, he will do so but in his time, not yours." She lowered her eyes back to her crocheting. "Minding our own business is the best way, ja?"

Frustrated, Anna didn't reply. She knew that Miriam was correct but that didn't stop her from being concerned. Something was bothering Steve and no one seemed to care. No one, she realized, except herself.

Chapter 5: Lizzie's Letter

Dear Family,

Seems strange to write a letter knowing that I will see all of you next week at sister Leah's for church. Sure do wish I lived closer so that we could come help prepare the house and food for the glorious day. Still, we are all looking forward to worshipping the Lord together, enjoying fellowship, and catching up in person.

Abraham and the boys have been busy working in the fields. We had a cow get caught up in a fence and that left quite a mess in the pasture. Cow should recover...just some scratches on her legs from the wire.

Our Susan is finally old enough to go on a camping trip with some of the other girls from her youth group. She's most excited about that. Not certain how she will feel after spending a few days living in a tent and cooking over a fire pit!

The little ones are keeping busy helping with the gardens. Canned seventy jars of beets last weekend. Rachel Ann wore most of the beet juice by the end of the day. Good thing she was wearing her work apron! Will be sending some of the cans to market with Sylvia.

I sure did enjoy reading everyone's letters. Wish I had more exciting news to write, but more than anything, I sure hope this letter finds all of you safe, happy, and full of God's grace.

Blessings and love to all of you.

Lizzie, Abraham, and the kinner

The buggies were parked along the driveway and a sea of men in black lingered in the morning sun. They spoke softly, catching up on the most recent happenings throughout the church district. Despite the good weather, most of the men in the community were farmers and that meant that the days were spent working with the dairy cows and crops. There wasn't a lot of time for visiting during the summer months.

The three-hour church service would begin promptly at nine o'clock. So people took advantage of arriving early to share the latest news. At today's service, all eyes were searching for Menno Yoder to arrive. When Mary Ruth showed up with the four *kinner* in hand, the men clicked their tongues and shook their heads. Once again, Menno Yoder was missing.

With voices lowered, the men expressed their concern for their neighbor.

"How long can he keep avoiding people?" one man asked.

"He needs to come back to church, to mingle with the folk and seek God's help," another replied.

Elijah stood with a group of men and listened to their concerns. He covered his mouth when he coughed, still fighting the flu for the past few weeks. It wasn't getting better and several men raised an eyebrow at him.

"Had that cough a while, Elijah," an older man named Benjamin said while tugging at his white beard thoughtfully. "Best go be seeing a doctor, I reckon."

Elijah nodded. "Ja," he said. "Rachel's been after me for the past week or so, Benjamin. Best be listening or her tongue will never stop wagging."

The men chuckled and nudged him. Elijah laughed with them, softening his teasing remark.

"Ain't your sister-in-law helping that Menno with his

kinner?"

Again, Elijah nodded. In truth, he hadn't seen much of Mary Ruth in the past few weeks. She was too busy helping the Yoder's as well as Leah, although he often wondered why Leah needed so much help. "Rachel keeps me updated. Says he's still fighting mad over Martha's death. Ignores the *kinner*. Yells at Mary Ruth. Bad situation, that."

"Yells at her? You don't say," Benjamin said, a frown on his face. "Don't sound much like Menno Yoder."

The other men grunted and nodded their heads in agreement. That much was true. Menno Yoder had always been a kindly man, eager to lend a hand to help neighbors in time of need. He was also very involved with the children, leading youth group gatherings throughout the year.

"It'll take some time to get used to his *fraa* passing," Elijah said softly. "Only been a month or so."

Anna was busy in the kitchen, helping the women with dishing out the prepared food for the noon meal. Dinner after the service was a wonderful time of fellowship. There would be two seatings today since there were so many guests that had attended the service a Leah's house.

The men had quickly transformed the church benches into long tables and the women were busy setting out plates, utensils, and cups. No napkins adorned the table. Younger women helped carry the different plates of food over to the table, setting them down at each section. There was sliced ham, bowls of chow-chow, bread, butter, and cup cheese with pretzels. All of the food had been prepared in advance and, while light fare, it was always a pleasant meal.

The first group of people sat down at the tables. Men were

on one side of the room while women were on the other side. The bishop stood before the table and gestured for the silent prayer before the meal. All heads bowed, eyes shut, as each person thanked God for the bounty of food that was before them. The silence in the room was magical, an instant of awe for the Lord and His gifts. Then, just as quickly, each head lifted and the room was filled with chatter and conversation among the different people, both seated and those serving them.

One woman walked up to Anna and smiled at her. "I'll take those dishes for you," the woman said. She was a pretty woman with dark hair and eyes that flashed. There was something about her smile that seemed familiar but Anna couldn't recall meeting her before this day.

When the woman walked away, Anna leaned over to Rachel and whispered, "Who was that woman?"

Rachel looked up from the ice chest where she was pulling out plates of wrapped cold cuts. "Who?" she asked, shutting the lid to the ice chest with her foot. She followed Anna's gaze and noticed the young woman, setting the plates that she had taken from Anna, onto the table before the men. "That's Mimi Hostetler," she said. "Why?"

For some reason, Anna found herself watching the young woman. "The name doesn't sound familiar but I feel like I should know her," Anna said softly.

"Ja, vell, her daed owns the farm store down the way a bit," Rachel said.

As Rachel was finishing her sentence, Anna noticed that Mimi Hostetler paused, just momentarily, next to where Steve sat, beside Elias. Despite being a bachelor, his age permitted Steve to eat with the first round of men, the older men, while the younger, unmarried men usually ate during the second seating. Rachel nudged Anna's arm but Anna continued to watch. Curious, Rachel followed Anna's gaze.

In that moment, Steve looked up at Mimi and smiled. It was a soft smile and his eyes glowed as they met her gaze. Mimi returned the smile and set down the plates that she had been carrying to the table right in front of Steve. Anna caught her breath and felt her own heart lurch inside of her chest.

"I wonder…" she whispered.

Rachel frowned. "Means nothing, Anna. Don't get silly ideas in your head now," she scolded. But Anna could tell that Rachel was also curious about that brief interaction they had just witnessed.

"Which store does her daed own?" Anna asked, fighting the rising color that threatened to turn her cheeks crimson under the scolding from Rachel.

"Hostetler's Farm Store," Rachel said sternly. "We have enough to worry about with John David and that Ella Riehl. No need to carry on about Steve. He's an old bachelor man now. One smile means nothing."

Anna sighed. She was so hopeful that Steve would still have that chance to find the companionship and love that she shared with Isaac. But she knew that wishing was not the same thing as God's will and it was only God's will that mattered.

"Where's Mary Ruth?" Anna said, changing the subject.

With a nod of her head, Rachel indicated the far table. Sure enough, there sat Mary Ruth with the other young mothers, surrounded by their *kinner*. For a moment, Anna frowned. "I don't understand," she said. "Why is she…?" But as the words came out of her mouth, she realized that Mary Ruth was tending to the Yoder children. Despite the fact that Menno Yoder had not seen fit to attend the worship service, three of his four *kinner* were there, seated around Mary Ruth. "I don't believe it!" she gasped and turned to look at Rachel. "What is this?"

This time, Rachel laughed. "I wouldn't have believed it

either," she said, "But our Mary Ruth has finally started to learn how to nurture."

"The Yoder children?" she asked in disbelief.

Rachel nodded. "The Yoder children."

"Isn't there a boy?"

Rachel glanced around the room and saw him standing alone by the wall. He was too old to sit with the women and, without his daed there, he probably felt uncomfortable sitting with the men. "Over there," she said and pointed. "Best be seeing that he gets a plate, ja?"

With a shake of her head, Anna felt her heart break once again for the Yoder children. Just remembering what the boy had witnessed made her want to cry. No child should lose a parent but especially not the mamm. "I'll send Katie over with a platter," she volunteered. "I seem to recall they spoke a bit at the funeral service fellowship."

She scanned the tables for Katie and noticed that she was seated next to Lovina, their brother James' wife. And next to Lovina sat Leah. A frown crossed Anna's face. It was not customary for the hosting family to eat during the first seating. Why on earth would Leah be seated at the table when the other women were busy tending to the kitchen needs?

"Don't say what you're thinking," a voice said in her ear.

Startled, Anna turned around in time to dodge her sister-in-law, Lizzie, who was storming past with her large arms laden with food. She watched as Lizzie pounded the floor to the tables, swooping down the different plates of food and plopping them onto the table. Lizzie was never one to back down from a challenge and Anna watched in amazement as Lizzie paused just momentarily beside her sister, Leah. Bending over, Lizzie whispered something into Leah's ear to which Leah flushed and responded with her mouth moving quickly and her hands waving in the air. She pointed to the baby seated on her lap but Lizzie shook her head before returning to the kitchen.

"That Leah," Lizzie scowled as she stomped back into the kitchen. "Never was one any lazier than that sister of mine."

"Lizzie!" Anna gasped at Lizzie's harsh words.

"Oh, I'll pray for forgiveness later," she snapped and waved her hand at Anna. "Bet that's why Mary Ruth is tending to those children so much…to escape Leah and her laziness!"

This time it was Rachel who laid a hand on Lizzie's arm. "Now Lizzie," she said calmly. "You know that she has her own issues dealing with baby Jacob."

"Baby Jacob? He's no more special needs than Leah is!" She glanced at Anna who stifled a nervous laugh. "Oh, I'll pray for forgiveness for that, too," Lizzie added. "But it's true! That child is an angel. Never fusses, rarely cries. Leah needs to pull it together for her other *kinner* and her husband, too!"

"Are you suggesting that our sister is taking advantage of our willingness to help out?" Rachel asked in a forthcoming tone.

"Ja, and then some!" Lizzie snapped back. "That's one of the reasons why I wouldn't come help her clean. She probably waits all year for worship service to appeal to others to come and properly tend to the needs of her home; and you know it, Rachel!"

"Girls!" Anna whispered. "Don't make a scene, please." She glanced around, too aware that there were many other women bustling about the kitchen with ears wide open to the Amish grapevine. There was no secret about Leah's inaptitude for housekeeping but to start a bicker session about it at Leah's house at the worship service meal? "For now, this is not the time or place, ain't so?"

Leaving the two women staring at each other in a silent face-off, Anna scurried over to the table and approached her daughter. She knelt down and tapped Katie on the shoulder.

"*Dochder*," she said softly. "When you are finished, could you come help me?"

"Ja, Mamm," Katie said, her eyes wide. "I can help clean the dishes if you need."

"*Nee*," Anna said with a gentle shake of her head. "I'd like you to take a plate to Melvin Yoder. He seems a bit lost and I'd hate for him to be hungry today." She glanced up and caught Mary Ruth's eye. There was a look of relief in her youngest sister-in-law's expression. She was holding the youngest Yoder child and helping to feed her while the other two girls clung to her side.

With Menno Yoder's family located in a church district too far away to come help on a regular basis, it was up to his own neighbors to step up and see him through his troubled times. Martha Yoder's death had been a tragedy, that was for sure and certain. But Anna could see now how much of the burden had fallen on Mary Ruth's shoulders.

Everyone else had moved along with their own lives during the week. After all, animals needed feeding and milking while crops needed tending. Of course, the evening meal was often brought in by different women in the community while on the weekends, people visited with Menno and the children. But during the week, Mary Ruth was becoming the primary caregiver during the workweek. She was too young to be burdened with this responsibility and Anna made a mental note to discuss this with Isaac, Elias, and Miriam.

She returned to the kitchen to prepare a plate for Melvin. Rachel and Lizzie were beginning to wash dishes in Leah's sink while several other women began to refill dishes of food for the second seating. Anna grabbed a towel and began to dry the dishes as fast as her two sister-in-laws could wash them.

"Elijah's headed to a doctor this week," Rachel said, her voice flat but the stress clearly apparent.

Looking up from the sink, Lizzie stared at her sister. "You

don't say?" Lizzie asked. "Whatever for? He looks fit as a fiddle."

Something flashed in Rachel's expression that wasn't lost on either Lizzie or Anna. It was as if a dark shadow passed before her. For that moment, she looked far away and removed from the situation. "It's his cough," she said. "Just won't go away. Never heard of a flu lasting this long, especially without fever. And he's always so tired."

Lizzie glanced over Rachel's shoulder to meet Anna's eyes. No words needed to be shared between them. The look was enough. If Elijah was going to the doctor and Rachel was supporting it, something was clearly wrong. "It's just a cough, nee?"

With a simple shrug, Rachel stared straight ahead while washing the dishes. "I reckon," she said. And with that, the conversation was over.

The first seating was over and the younger women began to hustle around the tables collecting silverware, cups, and plates that needed washing. The kitchen was a flurry of activity that, on first glance, would seem chaotic and disorganized, but on closer inspection, moved in a rhythmic flow. Clearly everyone knew what needed to be done and how to do it without asking for directives or getting in each other's way.

Leah hurried over, baby Jacob on her hip. She huffed and jostled him as she approached the sink. "Lizzie," she snapped. "I'm finished and can take over here if you're willing to tend to baby Jacob." She held the baby out as if passing a sack of potatoes.

She was surprised to see Lizzie shake her head. "You get one of the girls to tend to Jacob while you help. Those *dochders* of mine would be more than glad to help. They dote on your boppli and are more than capable, Leah." Lizzie stared over her sister's head, searching the room for her oldest daughter. When she caught Susan's eye, she motioned for her daughter to come and pointed to the baby in Leah's arms.

For a moment, Leah looked as though she would talk back and argue with Lizzie. What could a young girl know about tending a special needs baby? One with Downs Syndrome?, but with a stern glare cast in Leah's direction, Lizzie dared her to speak back against her suggestion.

Rachel chuckled as Leah hurried off, looking for one of Lizzie's daughters. For some reason, they were all too aware that Leah was reluctant to leave the boppli with anyone else. She cradled that child from sunrise to sunset, barely letting anyone hold him. It was as if she thought they would break the infant. But Lizzie had a way with Leah and, for that, Rachel was grateful.

"Need to see more of you, Lizzie," Rachel said. "Gets tiresome dealing with this all by myself."

Flapping her hand in the air, Lizzie dismissed her. "Never known you to be one to stand down to anyone, especially our younger sister," she stated.

"Speaking of younger sisters," Rachel started. "I'm surprised that Sylvia didn't attend today. It's rare to have everyone together but I thought they might show up."

Before Lizzie could respond, Leah returned and quickly accessed the kitchen. The other women were busy helping and Leah took a loud breath, taking charge of her own kitchen at last. "You ladies go eat now," she said with a forced smile. "Thank you for letting me tend the *kinner* but I can take over now," she added, a little too loudly for Anna's taste.

As the sister-in-law that lived with Miriam and Elias, Anna had always felt a little on the outside of the sisters. After all, they had grown up together, living on the very farm where Anna now raised her children. And the sisters were different. For the most part, they were confident and firm in their convictions, the only exception being Leah. Anna suspected that they were closer to each other than to Miriam. That suited Anna just fine, especially since she looked to Miriam as a second mother.

She felt relieved when Lovina approached her. Having shared the first seating with the other women, Lovina was now ready to assist so that these women could enjoy some food and conversation.

Lovina was a shy young woman who, Anna suspected, also felt as though she lived in the shadows of the other sisters. James was the second oldest son but had married later in life, taking on a younger bride who made his eyes sparkle. But no one had been able to get too close to Lovina. They lived further away from the other families and it was on a rare occasion that they traveled to visit. James' dairy farm was too time consuming to permit many social visits.

"Such a treat to see you!" Anna said with genuine feeling toward her sister-in-law. She had always suspected that, if Lovina lived closer, they would have formed a stronger friendship.

"*Danke*," Lovina said softly. Then, lifting her eyes, so brown and doe-like, she looked at Rachel and Lizzie. "How many I help?"

Ignoring Leah's huff at being passed over in her own house for instruction, Lizzie pointed toward the sink. "Best be washing those plates. Second seating is just about ready. Leah, you could help, ja?"

Anna saw the look of panic in Lovina's eyes. Lovina was too shy to stand up against Leah. That was a known fact. Leah would bulldoze her with directions and instructions, happy to finally have someone that was intimidated by her. "I'll help Lovina," Anna quickly volunteered. Then, with a smile at Leah, she added, "Besides, I'm sure Leah will want to direct the passing of the desserts, ja?"

Lovina and Anna washed the plates silently at first, creating a quick assembly line for scraping, washing, rinsing, and drying. It didn't take long for the room to begin to clear out. The younger children were outside playing in the yard. Mothers with young babies were nursing in the sunshine while catching up on the latest news. The unmarried youth were seated now, enjoying their midday meal. And the men were standing along the periphery, talking amongst each other.

"Is it true?" Lovina asked quietly. "About Eleanor Haile and the horses?"

For a moment, Anna didn't understand the question. Why would Lovina care about Eleanor Haile, she wondered. "You mean that she's boarding them at the Miller farm behind Menno Yoder's place?"

"Heard little Katie is going to be riding one of her ponies," Lovina answered. "Does that mean Eleanor Haile will be around more often, then?"

"I reckon so," Anna answered, choosing her words carefully. She was still puzzled as to why Lovina would know or care about Eleanor Haile. The expression on Lovina's face was equally puzzling: she looked openly concerned. "Eleanor's coming down this week, I'm told, and Katie will be going out to the farm to ride for the first time. If it goes well, Isaac said the pony could come back to our farm so that Katie can ride it more and take care of it." She handed a dish to Lovina. "Time she learned more responsibility."

As if on cue, Katie appeared beside her mamm and tugged gently on her dress. She stared up at her mamm with big eyes and waited patiently for Anna to dry her hands on her apron. "You have that plate for Melvin, ja?" Katie asked.

"Over there," Anna said, pointing to the counter. The plate had been set aside and was covered with a plain towel. "I think I saw him slip outside. Might be in the barn with the other *kinner*."

Katie nodded and reached for the plate. Hesitating, she turned back for a fork and knife. She noticed that Anna smiled at her, clearly impressed with Katie's thoughtfulness. Ever since her daed had agreed to the pony, Katie had been trying...really trying…to hold up her end of the bargain, even before Eleanor had actually picked her up to go riding.

Only four days, she told herself. Four days until she could meet her new pony and spend time caring for its mane, hooves, and tail. She couldn't wait to groom it, to hug it, to breathe in its earthy scent.

She found Melvin Yoder sitting on the back porch. It looked out over the fields toward his own daed's farm. Her feet stopped moving as she watched him, wondering if that was the field where his mamm had died. A shiver crawled up her spine. *Where his mamm died in front of him*, she thought. Swallowing back the lump in her throat, she forced back the tears. It made her so sad to think of Melvin Yoder without his mamm. No, she corrected herself. *Anyone without a mamm* made her sad.

"Melvin?" she said softly, not wishing to startle him. "My mamm sent me with some food. Reckon you'd be hungry, ja?"

He turned around, his face pale with dark circles under his eyes. It took him a moment to recognize her, especially since it had been well over a month since they had met at the funeral. But when she smiled at him, a soft smile that was full of understanding, he remembered her as Mary Ruth's niece, the one who had been so kind to him at his mamm's service.

Without a word, he took the plate and moved over so that Katie could sit next to him. He remained silent as he ate, slowly picking at his food with his fork. Katie watched him for a minute, torn between returning inside to help the women and staying here to keep Melvin company. When he glanced up at her, the sorrow so deep in his eyes, she decided against leaving him.

"Heard my *aendi* is helping out at your place," she said to break the silence.

He nodded.

"That going well, then?"

He shrugged.

Katie sighed. She wasn't certain of what to say to Melvin. The other children seemed to avoid him, as if he carried a disease. The dying mamm disease, she thought wistfully. She had noticed that at the funeral and she had noticed it today. Even his sisters clung to Mary Ruth and none of the other little girls approached them to play. With school being out for the summer, Melvin must sure be lonely, she realized.

"I'm getting a pony," she blurted out. "It's being boarded at your neighbor's farm, the Millers."

He frowned and looked at her. "That's awful far for you, ain't so?" he asked.

"My mamm's friend is going to be bringing me there on Thursday. You want to come ride with me?" She wasn't certain from where the question came, but as soon as it was out there, she was glad that she had asked it. Maybe a friend was what Melvin needed and she wasn't afraid that his misfortune would rub off on her. No, she told herself. My mamm isn't going to die, too!

"I..." He paused and looked down at his plate. He seemed to be contemplating the food, pushing at it with his fork once again. Then, with a deep breath, he looked up and met her eyes. "Ja, Katie Fisher, I would like that," he said. "I reckon it's time to move on a bit. *Danke* for asking me."

This time, Katie smiled a wide smile. There was something about Melvin Yoder. She wasn't certain if it was his dark eyes, so full of sorrow or the hint of life returning to them, but she was awful glad that her mamm had thought to ask her to bring him some food. Even more, she was glad she had decided to visit with him and she was looking forward to spending more time with him on Thursday.

Mary Ruth gathered up the Yoder *dochders* and looked around for Melvin. She saw him walking along the fence line in the field with little Katie tagging along beside him. Holding Emma Yoder's small hand, Mary Ruth stood up and watched. Melvin and Katie were deep in discussion as they walked, looking far too grown up for their young ages, but for a second, Mary Ruth thought she saw Melvin smile at Katie and it warmed her heart. It had been too long in coming, that smile of his.

"Suzanna" Mary Ruth said firmly but with tenderness in her voice. "Mayhaps you could go pick up the plates that I brought? I left them in a basket by the back door. There's a piece of blue thread tied to the handle so you'll know it's mine."

Obediently, Suzanna scurried away, her younger sister Ruth Ann tagging along, as they went to hunt for the basket. Mary Ruth smiled down at Emma. "Guess we should be getting back home to your daed, ja?"

Emma stuck her thumb in her mouth and looked away.

When the two other girls returned, Suzanna handed the basket to Mary Ruth. "Your sister, Rachel, packed it with food for daed," she said softly.

Mary Ruth smiled. "That was right kind of her, ja?" She took a deep breath and started walking down the driveway toward the Yoder's farm. She glanced over her shoulder at Melvin and Katie, deciding it was best to let the two enjoy each other's company, rather than drag Melvin home to the house of doom and gloom.

She was surprised to find Menno sitting on the front porch when they turned down the lane. He was dressed in his Sunday outfit and staring at his clasped hands. Hesitating, Mary Ruth watched him for a minute. She had never seen him looking so peaceful. He was still and silent. For a moment, she wondered if he was praying.

When Emma sneezed, Menno's concentration was broken.

He looked up and stared at the four of them. Bracing herself for another screaming match, Mary Ruth felt the tension in the back of her neck. Please God, she prayed. Not now. Not today.

So when he forced a weak smile and lifted a hand, a gesture of greeting, she frowned, wondering what was happening. He stood up and pressed the creases out of his pants. Then, straightening his hat on his head, he walked toward them.

"Mary Ruth," he said, acknowledging her with that simple greeting accompanied with a nod of his head. Then, turning his attention to his daughters, he bent down and reached for Suzanna's hand. "I was waiting for you to return from church," he said. His voice had a softer tone than usual.

Mary Ruth took a few steps backward, watching the scene unfold and giving them some privacy. It surprised her to see Menno speak softly to his *dochders*, caressing their hands and arms as if to comfort them. She lifted her hand to rub her throat, holding back the emotion that rose within her. Could it be, she thought, that God had finally answered her prayers and helped Menno get over his grief?

After a few minutes talking to the girls, Menno stood up and turned to face Mary Ruth. "And Melvin?" he asked.

"Ja, vell…" She found herself stumbling over her own words, as he stared at her. The change in Menno Yoder was astonishing and she hadn't been prepared for the transformation. "He's back at Jonah and Leah's, visiting with the other children."

For a moment, she thought she saw something dark pass through his expression, but, just as quickly, it changed and he nodded his head. "*Gut*," he said. "It is *gut* for him to be with some young friends."

They stared at each other for just a moment, Mary Ruth assessing the new Menno and not quite sure what to make of him while Menno stared at her, wondering how to apologize for his past behavior. Neither spoke, uncomfortable in the shift in their relationship.

Wanting to return home, Mary Ruth made the first move. She lifted her hand, holding the basket out toward Menno. "My sister prepared you some food for the evening meal," she said. "You were missed at worship service."

"I tried," he stated, gesturing toward his clothing. "But I'm not ready."

"Bishop will be stopping here later, I reckon. I'll ask him to bring Melvin," she said, taking another step backward. "Best be returning. Leah will need my help cleaning, that's for sure and certain." She thought she saw a hint of a smile on his face but it disappeared just as quickly.

"*Danke*," he said softly. "For bringing the girls back to me. I wasn't certain how to get them."

Mary Ruth frowned. "Someone would have bought them. I picked them up. Surely you knew I'd bring them back or arrange for a neighbor to do so."

He shrugged, shifting the basket in his arms. He glanced at his three daughters and spared them a rare smile. "Got some catching up to do," he said, reaching down with his free hand to hold Emma's in his. Mary Ruth fought a stab of jealousy. Hadn't Emma just been clinging to her own hand, not five minutes ago? Hadn't Suzanna and Ruth Ann been stuck to her side for the past month? Now, she was forgotten and their daed was all stars and sparkles in their eyes.

The walk back to Leah's took longer than she remembered as she battled the emotions that conflicted in her heart.

It was close to two o'clock and most of the church members had departed from Jonah and Leah's farm, returning to their own farms for afternoon activities of leisure such as playing

Scrabble or visiting with other family members. The rest of the Fisher family remained behind, helping Leah clean up from the gathering. The men sat outside on the porch, sipping at meadow tea and discussing farm related activities while the women reorganized the inside of Leah's kitchen and gathering room. Outside, the children ran and played, their laughter ringing through the air like the chatter of happy sparrows.

Miriam sat at the table, holding baby Jacob. She cooed at him, laughing when he smiled back at her. Leah was helping at the sink but continually glanced over her shoulder as if to assure herself that Jacob was just fine and not missing her.

Passing by her sister, Lizzie nudged Leah with her elbow. "The boppli's fine, Leah. Stop hovering so!"

Leah frowned and splashed some water at Lizzie, which caused Rachel and Anna to laugh. Lovina remained serious, feverishly drying the remaining dishes, her mind clearly elsewhere.

"What's bothering you, Lovina?" Lizzie asked, never one to beat around the bush. "You've been quiet as a mouse for the greater part of the day!"

At the question, Miriam looked up and watched her daughter-in-law, waiting for an answer. But Lovina merely smiled, a meek smile at that, and shook her head. "Not feeling too well, t'is all."

The room remained silent, a darkness hovering over the gathering. It was not a comfortable silence, all eyes watching Lovina. Her face was pale and taunt, clearly stressed about something. And the women didn't have to guess about what.

"It will happen if God wills it," Rachel said kindly, laying a hand on Lovina's arm. It seemed to be all that anyone could say to Lovina, Rachel thought. She wished she had some other words of wisdom but she knew of nothing else to say.

Nodding her head, Lovina kept her attention on the dishes.

She didn't reply. She didn't have to for they all knew what she was thinking. *If God wills it.*

The door opened and Mary Ruth breezed into the kitchen. She started to shut the door behind her, but as if an afterthought, decided to leave it open. The breeze would help cool the kitchen. "My word," she said as she collapsed on the bench next to her mother. She leaned over and peered at baby Jacob. He reached out a hand to touch her face. "Menno Yoder was on the porch when I dropped the girls off," she said, touching Jacob's hand and playing with his fingers. "He was actually pleasant."

Rachel raised an eyebrow. "Really?"

"Ja," Mary Ruth affirmed, "If you can imagine such a thing!"

"Now, now," Miriam scolded gently. "He always was a kindly man. Losing his wife in such a manner is bound to be hard on a soul. We need to pray for him, not judge him."

Mary Ruth made a face. "*Nee,* we need to pray for him to tend his own *kinner* because I want to come home!"

"Mary Ruth!"

She turned to look at her oldest sister who was staring at her with a shocked expression. "It's true! I'm tired of sleeping in a strange bed and not having decent meals."

Leah gasped.

"Oh please, Leah," Mary Ruth snapped. "We all know that you didn't inherit Mamm's cooking ability."

"Or cleaning," mumbled Lizzie.

"Girls!" Miriam snapped. She scowled at Mary Ruth. "And on a Sunday!"

Mary Ruth rolled her eyes and turned her attention back to Rachel. "He was dressed for Sunday service," she said, changing the subject away from Leah and back to Menno Yoder. "Said he wasn't ready yet. But he paid some attention to the girls."

"Gut, gut," Rachel said, nodding her head. "It's time for him to start healing."

Lizzie nodded her head. "You've been doing a *gut* thing, Mary Ruth, tending to those children." She moved to put some of the dried dishes back in the cabinet next to Lovina. "A right *gut* thing," she added as she shut the cabinet door.

"They're going to miss you when you return to Mamm's," Rachel added.

"And when, exactly, might that be?" Mary Ruth dared to ask.

Leah reared her head, her eyes wide and full of questions. "I thought you were supposed to be here to help me with baby Jacob!"

"Oh Leah," Lizzie sighed. "The last thing you need is help. In fact, it would do you some good to not have help and get back on your feet. That child is as golden as an angel and about as much bother as one."

"I don't appreciate that," Leah said, her tone low and sulky.

"It's the right honest truth!"

Ignoring her bickering sisters, Mary Ruth looked up at the sound of footsteps on the front porch. She stood and hurried to the window, peering outside. Melvin and Katie stood on the porch, throwing a stick for the dog to fetch. "Didn't realize Melvin was still here," she said softly and hurried away from the commotion that lingered in the kitchen.

The screen door opened with a screech, obviously in desperate need of some oiling. Mary Ruth shut it behind herself and cleared her throat to announce her presence to the two children who were now squatting at the edge of the porch, poking at the dirt with a stick.

When Melvin looked up, Mary Ruth caught her breath. For

the first time, she realized how much Melvin favored his father in his appearance. She hadn't noticed it before, especially with Menno always scowling and yelling at her. But this afternoon, when he had tried to force some civility toward her, his appearance also seemed to change. Now that Melvin's face had taken on a softer look with less sorrow in his eyes, the resemblance was undeniable.

"I already walked your sister's home," Mary Ruth said gently, her eyes softening as she smiled at Melvin.

"Katie asked me to go riding ponies on Thursday," he gushed. "May I?"

"Ponies?" Mary Ruth asked, looking from one child to the other. She had heard about Eleanor Haile boarding those ponies at the Miller farm and seemed to recall something about Katie with one of those ponies from a discussion not so long ago, but truth be told, she had forgotten all about it. "Why, that sounds like a right fun thing to do, doesn't it?" she said, pleased to see the eagerness in his expression. "But you have to ask your daed, Melvin. He would make the decision on that, ja?"

Something suddenly changed on Melvin's face, like a cloud passing over his eyes. The eagerness disappeared and the spirit retreated back inside of him. Immediately, Mary Ruth realized her mistake. Melvin was just as fearful of Menno as she was herself; fearful of his emotions and outbursts; fearful of his mourning. Left to his own devices, Melvin would never ask his daed for permission.

"But," Mary Ruth said slowly, dreading the promise she was about to make. "I reckon I could speak to your daed for you," she offered carefully. The smile immediately returned to his face, the look of distress replaced by a wave of relief. If he wanted to say something, he didn't have time because she looked toward the men standing near the barn. "Now, let's see about getting you a ride back to your home, ja? Mayhaps Steve can take you."

It was thirty minutes later when Steve was pulling out of the Yoder farm. He had happily volunteered to take young Melvin home and hurried to hitch up his daed's buggy to the horse. The ride to the Yoder farm was quiet. Melvin didn't seem inclined to say much. But Steve was thankful that Mary Ruth hadn't volunteered to ride along. He had something else in mind before returning to Jonah and Leah's.

Instead of turning the horse left onto the lane, he turned right and headed toward the Hostetler home. It was only two miles from the Yoder's farm and Steve was fairly certain that Mimi had gone directly home with her parents. He hadn't managed to speak to her at the worship service and didn't think he'd be able to get back to the area later that evening. Make hay while the sun shines, he told himself. And it didn't hurt that Lizzie had brought out some cinnamon minis, protected in a Tupperware container to drop off at the Yoder's. Mayhaps, he thought, he'd just forget to drop them off at the Yoder's. Use that as his excuse why he was late returning to Leah's home.

When he pulled into the Hostetler farm, he hesitated. What would Mimi think, he wondered, that he had arrived unannounced?

"Well hullo there!" someone called from the shed.

Steve turned around and saw Mimi's father. He greeted him with a friendly handshake and glanced over his shoulder. "Was looking for your *dochder*," he said. "Just to have a word with her."

Jonas Hostetler raised an eyebrow and hid a smile. "You don't say, ja?" He motioned toward the house. "Reckon she's in there, helping her mamm. You're welcome to go up to the door and ask for her."

Color rose to Steve's face and he nodded his appreciation for the invitation. Then, with his hands pushed into his pockets, he hurried toward the kitchen door. She was standing there, waiting for him, when he climbed the three porch steps. Pushing the door open, she greeted him with a big smile.

"Steve Fisher ! What a surprise!"

He felt the color painting his cheeks crimson. Had she really been surprised? Perhaps he shouldn't have come there after all. "Just wanted a word with you," he said softly, too aware that there were other people in the kitchen behind her. They were listening to every word, that was for sure and certain.

Mimi slipped out the door and stood before him, her hands clutched before her. "A word?"

He leaned over. "Wanted to see if you'd like to go for a ride one night this week," he asked.

"In a car or a buggy?" she teased.

"Buggy, of course," he shot back. She had made her position quite clear about courting in a car.

"You keep borrowing your daed's buggy," she pointed out lightly. "Mayhaps time to invest in one of your own." The rebuke was gentle but the point well made. For a moment, he felt his cheeks redden, knowing she was right. When she noticed the crimson color flushing his face, she quickly added, "I'd be happy to go riding with you, Steve Fisher." Lowering her voice, she smiled and said. "But you already knew that, ain't so?"

"Wanted to talk to you after fellowship, but you sure left awful quick," Steve said.

She glanced at the kitchen door behind her. Steve followed her gaze and noticed three older women seated at the table. The women were peering over each other, trying to see who was at the door. Mimi bit her lower lip and turned back to Steve. "My *aendi* and her friends are visiting," she explained softly. "Had to get home before they arrived."

For a moment, they were silent. With people watching,

Steve felt uncomfortable. Besides, he knew that he had to return to Leah's. His daed needed the buggy to return home and he still had to stop back at the Yoder's to drop off the cinnamon minis.

"Is Tuesday night a good evening, then?" he asked, taking a step backward.

She nodded her head, her eyes sparkling at him. "That sounds right nice, Steve."

He tried to hide his own pleasure at her reaction. There was something about Mimi Hostetler that made him feel as if he was six feet tall and full of God's glory. His mind was in a whirl and his heart fluttering. He had never felt such joy as when she turned her gaze upon him and smiled.

"Ja vell," he said, reluctantly. But he knew it was time to cut the visit short. "Best head back to Leah's. But I'll be back for you on Tuesday."

He gave her a last wave as he pulled his daed's buggy out of the driveway and headed back down the lane toward the Yoder's farm. His heart pounded inside his chest and he watched in the mirror on the side of the buggy, seeing her stand on the porch, staring after him.

Tuesday was going to seem an awful long time in coming, he thought. But the smile on his face and in his heart told him that Mimi Hostetler was well worth the wait!

Chapter 6: Sylvia's Letter

Dear Family,

Was sure sorry to have missed church service at Leah and Jonah's on Sunday but it was right nice to receive the package of letters from everyone. Made me feel as if I was all caught up on everyone's lives...almost as gut as being at the service. Thank you for including us.

Our Naomi is looking forward to the camping trip with Lizzie's Katie. She's been working so hard with the market that a little break for her is just what she needs. She can't wait.

The twins are growing so fast. Can't believe how time seems to fly with not just one but two little ones running under foot. I miss them terribly when I have to go to market but thank the good Lord that John's mamm is able to stay with them.

Looking forward to seeing Rachel and Leah this upcoming week for making applesauce in preparation of the winter months ahead.

May God bless each of you.
Sylvia, John and family

When Sylvia arrived at Rachel's home on Thursday morning, she was relieved to have a few hours without the twins. Her older children were tending them while she spent some time with her two older sisters. Of course, her husband John's mamm would be there, to keep an eye too. It was always good to have an adult around, especially with two toddlers in the house. Lord only knew what type of mischief they might get into, she thought with a frown on her face but a smile in her heart.

"Hullo?" she called out as she opened the door to Rachel's kitchen. They had agreed to make the applesauce at Rachel's house since Leah's tended to be a bit in disarray. Besides, having just hosted the church service on the previous Sunday, Leah didn't want to have another major cleanup to go through. They would make the applesauce in the morning and enjoy a lovely sisterly dinner at noon.

Sylvia set her two boxes of empty glass jars on the counter of the laundry room. Tucked inside that box was a large Tupperware container filled with her favorite lima bean and corn salad that everyone always begged her to bring. Her hand lingered on the edge of the boxes as she looked around. The house was quiet. No children running around. No voices. No laughter. A bit unusual, she reckoned. She frowned and called out again. "Rachel, you home?"

Someone coughed upstairs and she thought she heard footsteps. Sylvia walked through the doorway into the kitchen and stood at the bottom of the staircase and called out one last time. "Rachel? You upstairs?"

"Just a minute," her sister finally answered. Her voice was muffled, clearly from behind a closed door. A little unusual, Sylvia thought.

Frowning, Sylvia turned back toward the kitchen. No reason that she could not get a head start peeling some apples. She glanced around until her eyes fell upon several large boxes full of apples behind the kitchen door. Without hesitation, she hurried in that direction, bent over to pick up a box, and carried it to the sink.

Rachel's house was so orderly, just like Mamm's, so it was easy for Sylvia to find a good knife to start the peeling and coring of the apples. She was already on her third apple when she heard her sister walking down the wood steps. Sylvia glanced over her shoulder and smiled at Rachel. "Guder Mariye, sister!"

But Rachel didn't smile back. There was no joy in her expression or greeting. Indeed, her face appeared drawn and pale; there were dark circles under her eyes. Clearly something was wrong. Very wrong!

"Rachel?" Sylvia asked, the smile fading from her own lips as she realized that, whatever was wrong was a deep wrong. She set the half-peeled apple on the counter next to the knife and hurried over to her sister. "What is it? Are you feeling poorly?"

"*Nee*," Rachel whispered. She let her younger sister lead her toward the table and sat on a chair.

"What is it, then? Are you expecting?"

Shaking her head, Rachel frowned at the question. If only that was the issue, she thought wryly. "Nee, nee," she said sharply, waving her hand at her sister. "You ask too many questions, Sylvia."

Silence befell them. Sylvia didn't know what to say or do. She was afraid to speak, recognizing that her older sister was obviously not in the mindset to share what was wrong. Yet, she felt that it would be construed as heartless to just turn back to peeling the apples. She decided to continue asking.

"Rachel," she offered gently, reaching out to touch her older sister's arm. "Talk to me."

The soft tone of Sylvia's voice caused Rachel to look up. She stared at Sylvia's face for a long, quiet moment. Sweet Sylvia. She had always been the caring and tender one in the family. Unlike Lizzie and herself who were so strong headed and quick to take charge, Sylvia was the quiet one that always cared for the sick kittens or injured calves. *How will Sylvia try to heal this situation,* Rachel thought wryly. Immediately, she felt guilty for having thought something so less than kind about Sylvia.

Rachel cleared her throat. "It's Elijah," she confessed, her voice all but a whisper. "The doctor wants him to see a specialist for his cough."

This time, it was Sylvia who frowned. She couldn't understand why this would be such a serious matter to cause her sister to look as if the bottom of her world had just fallen away. "His...cough?"

Rachel nodded. "He's had that cough for several weeks, maybe even longer, now. We thought it was summer flu but it hasn't gone away. On Monday, he went to a doctor in town. They ran some tests." She paused, licking her lips, which felt dry and cracked. "I just got the message from the answering machine. The doctor gave us the name of an oncologist."

Sylvia gasped. "An oncologist? Isn't that a...?" But she stopped short in the middle of her sentence, unable to say the word.

"Ja, a cancer doctor," Rachel said the word for her. "He wants Elijah to see a *cancer* doctor!"

"That can't be! Elijah has always been so healthy!"

Rachel took a deep breath. "We'll be going next Wednesday. That was the earliest appointment we could get and I think our regular doctor had to ask for some special favors to get us in so soon."

Sylvia was stunned, speechless at what Rachel had just told her. Cancer! "Well," she started slowly. "They might just be sending him there as a precaution; to run some more tests and to rule it out, you know?"

To Sylvia's surprise, Rachel reached out and grabbed her younger sister's hand. That was quite unusual for her to reach out in that way. Her eyes seemed wild as she searched Sylvia's face. "You don't understand," she whispered. "I have a real bad feeling about this, Sylvia."

"Stop that," Sylvia replied, more because she was scared herself rather than offended by her sister's statement. "Don't say such things." She lowered her voice and held Rachel's hand, clutching it tightly in hers, then continued: "We must pray to God for help in dealing with this situation, not second guess His will, Rachel. That is the best way. Our way"

For a long moment, the two sisters, Rachel and Sylvia, sat alone in the kitchen, heads bent together as they held each other's hands and prayed: prayed that the doctors were wrong, prayed that Elijah would get better, and prayed that God would give them the strength to deal with the alternative.

Leah had been in rare form that morning. Rachel's children had crossed the road shortly after breakfast so that the older boys could watch Leah's children. Leah had fussed and carried on about leaving baby Jacob in the care of young boys. But Rachel had been quite clear about it: Leah must come alone for the applesauce canning. It was a time for the sisters to visit while working.

Mary Ruth had watched the scene with a combination of pity and amusement. It was too obvious that Leah was a nervous Nellie about anyone watching baby Jacob, fearing that his condition made him more fragile than other babies. Still, it was time for Leah to realize that more than one person could watch her infant son. For Leah to spend the morning with her sisters would do her some good, Mary Ruth was sure of that.

She was standing in Menno Yoder's kitchen, thinking about these things when Menno walked through the door. The children had already eaten breakfast and were upstairs tidying up their rooms and getting ready before it was time to help with chores around the house and farm. The clock on the wall ticked loudly and struck the half-hour chime. It broke the silence in the kitchen and she paused for just the quickest of moments to look out the kitchen window, her hand holding a plate that she had just dried as she studied the green leaves on a large tree by the barn. Soon the leaves would change and fall. Winter would be upon them and that was a depressing thought to Mary Ruth.

Unbeknownst to her, Menno stood in the doorway for a long moment, watching Mary Ruth. As she was contemplating the tree and its giant limbs with fluttering leaves, he was studying her. It wasn't until she put away the last of the breakfast dishes that he shook his head, too aware that the woman in the kitchen was not his Martha, his deceased wife. A pang of loneliness swept through him. But he realized that loneliness was better than anger. Perhaps he was beginning to heal, he thought.

When he cleared his throat, she jumped, startled at the noise. "Menno!" she exclaimed, her hand pressed against her chest. "I hadn't heard you come in!"

The widower smiled, but it was a small smile, one that was not full of happiness or joy. "I reckon not, the way you just jumped out of your skin!"

His smile struck her as odd. She didn't remember ever seeing him smile before. Or attempt to, she told herself. *A right gut sign.*

She shut the cabinet door and wiped her hands on her apron. "Did you eat breakfast, then?" she asked nonchalantly. "I fed the *kinner* already but I can make some more eggs and toasts right quick if you're hungry." She knew that he would most likely refuse so she didn't mind making the offer. He had yet to share a single meal that she had prepared in the five weeks that she had been helping out at the house, after Martha Yoder's accidental passing.

Menno didn't answer right away as his eyes trailed around the room. She wondered what he was looking at and, for the briefest of moments, she followed his gaze.

Everything was neat and tidy. The floors were clean and the windows free from dust and fingerprints. The sun shone through the glass panes creating a natural light in the room. Mary Ruth had made certain to not change anything in the house from the way that

Martha Yoder had kept it. Even the blanket that was tossed over the back of the sofa in the back sitting room was folded exactly as Martha used to do.

"Ja," he said softly.

His response surprised her and she wondered if she had heard him correctly. "Ja what?" she asked, not wanting to take the chance that she understood him properly.

But she had. He turned and looked at her. There was a gentle peace about his gaze that startled her. "I'll have some breakfast. That would be right gut, Mary Ruth."

Surprised, she quickly hurried about the kitchen, too aware that he had already taken a seat at the table. She wasn't used to him being a presence in the house. Especially around her. In fact, for the past five weeks, he had done everything to avoid her unless he was yelling at her about getting out of his house, when dealing with his initial anger following his wife's death. Now, he was seated at the table, waiting for a breakfast plate and a cup of coffee.

She felt nervous, wondering if he was going to criticize her method of cooking or making the coffee. She had never cooked before a man, at least not one that wasn't her daed or *bruders*. Trying to quell the pit in her stomach, Mary Ruth tried to focus as she pulled out the very pans that she had just cleaned and put away. Within minutes, she had bacon frying in one pan and scrambled eggs cooking in the other. She even had the toast crisping on a back burner. When everything was cooking nicely, she poured him a fresh cup of coffee and carried it to the table.

"I don't know how you like it," she admitted, feeling like she was talking to a complete stranger. Indeed, this new Menno was not the same man she had been dealing with for the last five weeks. Was he finally healing?

"Black is fine, *danke*," he replied.

Black, she thought. Just like her own daed.

"The children?" he asked as he raised the cup to his lips. He blew on it twice before tasting it. "Um, gut," he commented.

"Upstairs," she answered, turning back to the stove to push the eggs around before they'd stuck to the pan. "I thought to have the girls weed the garden this morning. Not certain about Melvin," she said. Something tugged at her memory as she said Melvin's name. What was it that she had forgotten?

"Sure could use some help from Melvin in the fields this afternoon," Menno said.

This afternoon? And then she remembered. "Ja, he wanted to go pony riding with my niece at the Miller farm this afternoon," she said casually. "But if you need him in the fields…"

"Nee, nee," Menno said quickly. "It would be right *gut* for him to spend time with your niece, ain't so? *Gut* to have a friend and some laughter in his life. Been enough sadness to go around for a lifetime." His voice trailed off at the last sentence and Mary Ruth swallowed, realizing that Menno had come a long way since that first day she had met him. Indeed, he was healing and that was a surely right *gut* thing for everyone.

It was later in the afternoon when Steve asked to borrow Isaac's buggy again. No one seemed to raise an eyebrow over the fact that Steve was borrowing it again and during the middle of the afternoon, at that. For the past few weeks, he had been borrowing the buggy quite frequently. While the family speculated as to what that could mean, no one seemed to question it.

It took but less than ten minutes for Steve to harness the horse to the buggy. While bridling the horse, he made a mental note that the overcheck connecting the bridle's crown piece to the harness saddle's hook was wearing thin and decided to replace it while visiting Samuel's carriage shop, the purpose of today's outing.

The carriage store was only five miles from the family farm. Steve had known Samuel Esh for his entire life and knew him to be a hardworking and honest man with a very good reputation within the community and beyond. Many of the youth purchased their courting buggies from him and Samuel had never let slip when they did. Steve knew that he could trust Samuel.

"Hullo there," Samuel greeted when Steve walked into the door of the shop.

Steve glanced around. The shop was open and full of light from the walls of windows. He could see that Samuel was busy working on several buggies, all with grey tops and large black wheels. "Looking for a buggy to buy," Steve said, his hands tossed in his pockets as he stared at the one closest to him. He tried to ignore the pounding of his heart inside of his chest. Was he really going to buy a buggy? *After all of these years*, he thought.

"Dat's gut! I sell buggies!" Samuel teased, wiping his hands on his pants. He paused and studied Steve for a moment as if trying to place his face. It only took a moment for the light of recognition to hit him. "You the Fisher boy, not?"

Steve flushed at being called a boy.

"Ain't seen you in here before," Samuel said, pulling at his beard as if that helped him remember. "You look a bit old for a courting buggy but don't have no beard, do you, now?"

"Not married," Steve admitted, suddenly hating the way that sounded.

"So you looking for a regular buggy then? Or open top?" Samuel Esh certainly didn't waste any time before he got right down to business. Steve wasn't certain if that was good or bad.

"Regular, I reckon," he said. "Won't be needing no courting buggy for long, anyway." Either she said yes or she didn't. But he wasn't about to be driving around in an open top buggy, regardless of her answer.

Samuel studied Steve for a moment as if making up his mind regarding some detail about the buggy. Finally, he clucked his tongue as if he had come to a decision. "Reckon this is your first buggy. Must be using a driver for most of your travels but you have an intention to take on a family now, ja?" He didn't wait for Steve to answer the question as he turned around and walked toward the back of the shop, motioning for Steve to follow.

"See what I have," he continued. "Back here."

Steve stepped around a beautiful new buggy with shiny black shafts and maroon interior. He wondered who was buying that beautiful buggy. But Samuel Esh led him to the very back of the shop and stopped before another buggy that wasn't quite finished.

"Young man was going to buy this one here, but cancelled the order," Samuel said, shaking his head disapprovingly. "Right *gut* buggy, too. Solid. Has those new fancy wheels that recharge the buggy battery while you drive. No need to be hauling the battery to the diesel machine to recharge it."

"You don't say?" Steve liked that idea, but realized that such a convenience also sounded expensive.

Samuel scratched at his beard. "Don't imagine he'd mind if I sold it to you instead, seeing that he cancelled the order and lost his deposit."

"He cancelled it?" Steve asked, wondering why anyone would do that.

"Ja, cancelled it. Seems his brother was buying a new one from Strasberg and sold him his old one." It was evident that Samuel Esh didn't think too much of that decision. "Take a look and see what you think."

Steve took a deep breath, not certain what he was looking

for in a new buggy. After all, to him, most buggies were the same. They had four wheels, two doors, and windows that opened in the front for the reins to come through and a pair of shafts to hitch to the horse. But he pretended to know what he was doing as he circled around the buggy. He slid the door open and peeked inside, pleased to see a dark, navy blue fabric over the seats.

"Nothing wrong with that buggy," Steve said. "When will it be finished?"

"If I have a buyer? Next week. Just need to paint the wheels and shafts, ja?"

"How much?" Steve asked.

"Was $6000," Samuel said.

Steve caught his breath at the figure. He hadn't expected it to be that much.

"But I'm willing to drop it to $5500," he said. "Want to get it out of my shop. Coming on fall time…not as many new buggies to be sold. I'll even throw in a new biothene harness for the horse."

Steve looked over at the buggy again. It was well made, that was for certain. And he knew that a well-taken care of buggy could last the best part of thirty years. It might be the only buggy that he'd ever need to buy, especially with that second seat in the back.

"Next week?" Steve asked, scratching at his neck.

"Ja. Just needs about six coats of paint on the wood there," Samuel said, pointing with his finger at the unpainted places. "Maybe by Friday if I get a deposit today." He winked at Steve. "Could start on the first coat this afternoon."

It was a tremendous amount of money but Steve knew that it was also a good investment. An investment in his future, he told himself. And Samuel Esh had one of the best reputations in the area. Certainly he was an honest businessman or else word would have circulated.

Just as quickly, he thought back to the previous Tuesday when he had picked up Mimi Hostetler in his brother's borrowed buggy. For the first time, he had actually felt a wave of shame in the fact that he had never purchased a buggy of his own and had to court his girl in someone else's. What message did that send, he wondered, to her parents who certainly were aware that their daughter was being courted by a man who didn't own his own horse and buggy? Would they wonder that he couldn't provide for Mimi, should it come down to that decision? The memory caused Samuel to feel a wave of guilt and remorse. Yes, he thought, buying a buggy now was truly an investment in tomorrow. That "sealed the deal" as the Englischer often said.

"All right then," he said and turned to look at Samuel, holding his hand out to shake the older man's. "Let's try for next Friday then, ja?" And with that, the deal was made.

Katie stared at the pony. It was cream colored with a fluffy white mane. Its large, dark brown eyes seemed to stare back at her, as if the two of them were quickly and quietly assessing each other. It was hard to see those chocolate colored eyes as its forelock hung over its face. But the pony seemed to be staring at her, watching her every move with great curiosity.

Katie was not very experienced with horses but she knew that they had the natural ability to sense the moods and intentions of their handlers and react accordingly. She tried to still her beating heart and stop her palms from sweating. Certainly she didn't want to pony to sense how nervous she was.

"Mine?" she asked softly, refusing to tear her eyes from the pony to look at Eleanor who stood by her side.

"You bet," the Englische woman answered, her voice cheerful and upbeat. "I'll need to borrow her back next summer for a spell, but you take good care of her in the meantime and I promise to return her to you in the fall."

Katie glanced over her shoulder at Eleanor. "What's her name, then?"

"Butterscotch," the woman said, reaching a hand out to stroke the pony's white mane. "And she's quite the good girl."

For a long moment, Katie felt as if she was dreaming. For years, she had wanted her own pony to love. Two of her friends had ponies and they rode those ponies everywhere during the warmer months. Katie sometimes watched, fighting the urge to feel envy for her friends. But it was hard to be so good that she didn't feel a touch of jealousy at their joy. Despite the fact that they let her ride their ponies, Katie knew it wasn't the same thing. She wanted her own pony, one that she could groom and feed and ride when she wanted to, not when she was granted permission.

"Butterscotch," she repeated softly. It was a right *gut* name, Katie thought. After all, the pony was the color of butterscotch ice cream, that was for sure and certain. "May I groom her?"

Holding up her hand, Eleanor waved a small bucket that she had hidden behind her back. "You sure can! I even brought you some grooming tools, Katie," she said. "Just in case you didn't have any to bring with you: A curry comb, a couple of hard brush, a body brush, a sweat scraper and a hoof pick. You may leave these here so you'll always have them handy."

A broad smile broke out onto Katie's face. Eleanor had sure thought of everything, she reckoned. Timidly, she reached out to take the bucket then turned back to the pony. *Butterscotch*, she thought, her heart racing with excitement. *My Butterscotch.*

There was a rattle in the driveway of the farm and Katie looked up in time to see a grey-topped buggy driving down the lane. It stopped outside of the open barn door. She squinted and tried to make out who had arrived. When she recognized Melvin climbing out of the buggy, she laughed and waved her hand. "Over here," she called. "We're inside, Melvin. Come see the new pony"

He greeted her with a big grin, quickly assessing the pony. "Wow," he said, whistling under his breath. "That's one nice looking pony."

Katie beamed.

"Does she drive at all?"

Not knowing the answer, Katie looked over at Eleanor who was leaning against the stall door. The Englische woman with long brown hair and frosted spice colored lipstick smiled at her. "I'm not quite sure," Eleanor admitted. "But you are welcome to give her a try on a pony cart."

A deep voice joined the discussion. "Try what?"

Eleanor glanced over her shoulder at the tall man that entered the barn. Beside him was Mary Ruth who looked even more petite next to the man. "Well, hullo there, Mary Ruth! What brings you here?" Smiling, she moved away from the stall door and quickly embraced her friend. "Come to check the ponies?"

"Oh ja," Mary Ruth nodded. She hadn't a choice in the matter. Melvin had been anxious all week, checking the calendar each morning to see when Thursday was coming. It was all that he could talk about. "Melvin wanted to see Katie's new pony," she explained. "His daed here was kind enough to give us a ride."

For a moment, Eleanor looked at Menno, taking in the sight of the man standing beside Mary Ruth. She had heard about the awful accident that had taken his wife's life and left him a widower, a few months ago. He was a tall man with thick black hair and sad eyes. Yet, despite the sorrow, he was a good-looking man. "I'm Eleanor Haile," she said, reaching her hand out to shake his.

He hesitated then grabbed her hand awkwardly. He was clearly uncomfortable meeting the young Englische woman. "Menno Yoder, Melvin's father" he said, his voice strained and stiff.

Mary Ruth turned to Menno and forced a smile. "*Danke*, Menno," she said. "I'll be certain to pick up the girls from Leah's when we walk back."

He nodded then turned, disappearing out the open barn door as he headed for his buggy without another word.

Eleanor frowned and looked at Mary Ruth who merely shrugged and turned her attention back to the pony.

"That's a right sweet pony," she said to her niece. "What's its name?"

"Butterscotch," Katie answered. Then, turning to Melvin, she waved him into the stall. "I'm going to groom her. Want to help?"

Mary Ruth stepped aside so that Melvin could open the stall door to join Katie. Eleanor motioned for Mary Ruth to move further into the shadows of the barn so that they could talk privately, out of the hearing of the two young children.

"Saw Anna today," Eleanor said, her voice low but a smile on her face. "I heard that sister Sylvia was headed to Rachel's today. Perhaps I could drive you over there after the children are finished?"

A smile broke onto Mary Ruth's face. She hadn't seen Sylvia in a long time. "Oh Eleanor!" she gushed. "That would be right gut. I don't know when I saw her last and she missed the church service at Leah's last weekend!"

"I thought as much," Eleanor said. She turned back to look at the children. Katie was showing Melvin how to use all of her grooming tools and, together, they were rubbing down Butterscotch's coat.

When Eleanor pulled her truck into Rachel's farm, Mary Ruth immediately felt a strange chill going through her spine.

Something was wrong, she thought. She could sense it. The farm was quiet. Too quiet. Yet there were four buggies parked in the driveway, the horses unhitched and tied to the posts by the barn.

Mary Ruth frowned and turned back to Eleanor. "This isn't right," she said. "No one is outside."

At Rachel's house, there were always children running around outside. Her farm was one that was always full of life and activity. Even if the children were playing out of sight, Elijah would be in the fields or barnyard with his older sons. After all, school hadn't started yet for the younger *kinner*.

Leaving Eleanor with Katie and Melvin, Mary Ruth hurried toward the front porch. She stepped over a scooter that was carelessly left lying on its side, blocking the sidewalk. There was laundry in a basket on the front porch, still wet and in need of hanging. Just another sign that something wasn't right, she thought.

"Hullo?"

She opened the side door and stepped into the mudroom. She could barely see inside the kitchen until she walked through the second doorway. There, seated around the table, Mary Ruth saw her sisters Rachel, Sylvia, and Leah as well as her mamm and Anna. For a moment, she was confused. She hadn't heard that her mamm and Anna were coming over, too.

"What's wrong?" she asked, moving quickly to the table and placing her hand on her mother's shoulder. "Mamm?"

It was clear that they had been talking about something serious. Their faces were drawn and pale. It was Anna who spoke on Rachel's behalf. "It's Elijah," she said softly. "The doctors think he has cancer."

"Oh no," Mary Ruth whispered. She felt as if the wind was knocked out of her. Elijah? How could something like this happen to such a wonderful, *gut* man? Cancer was serious, regardless of what kind. Cancer meant treatments and treatments meant he would be laid up and that meant fields and animals wouldn't be tended. That spelled disaster for the entire family.

Mamm shook her head. "Just doesn't seem right," she said, taking the words out of Mary Ruth's mouth.

Rachel wiped at her eyes. She had been crying. That was something that Mary Ruth hadn't seen too often with her oldest and strongest sister. Tears? "Well," Rachel said. "No use sitting here crying, I reckon." She started to stand up but her knees buckled. Steadying herself by holding the back of the chair, she looked around the room. "We have a lot of applesauce to make, ja? Best get started. The apples won't get peeled by sitting here worrying about what God has already determined and there is not anything we can do about it."

Everyone glanced up when the door opened again and Eleanor walked in, followed by Katie and Melvin. She smiled brightly at everyone until she saw everyone's expressions. Quickly, she realized that something had happened and the smile faded from her face.

"Everything OK?" she asked, her voice hesitating slightly.

Anna glanced at the *kinner* then looked back at Eleanor. "Ja, ja," she said, standing up. "Right as rain. Even better now that you are here to help peel apples." She tried to sound chipper and upbeat so that the *kinner* wouldn't get scared. A sick parent for one always created fear in the others.

Within minutes, Anna had taken charge of the applesauce making, putting Melvin, Katie, and Eleanor to work peeling the apples while she poured water into the large black cauldron that Rachel had already placed on the brick cooking stove. Anna gave them each a task and fussed over the children, keeping them busy so that the emotions in the kitchen could be isolated from their young hearts.

While the four of them worked together in the laundry

room over the wash sink and wood stove, the other women stayed in the kitchen, sharing the grief and dread that Rachel felt over the upcoming visit to the oncologist. When it was clear that the children were distracted, the women bowed their heads and said a silent prayer, each praying for a healthy prognosis at that doctor's meeting next week. It would be a long wait until that prognosis was made, that was for sure and certain.

Chapter 7: Lovina's Letter

Dear Family,

It has been a beautiful summer. What blessings we have received from the Lord with the weather. The kinner are happy, enjoying their days off from school although the older boys have been busy helping their daed in the fields. Harvey is right glad for the help. Sure makes his hay cutting days easier.

Church was at Silas Troyer's last Sunday and we had lots of visitors as Elsie Smucker turned 85 last weekend. Lots of nephews and nieces attended the service and we had a lovely cake for her after church. Having just moved in with her nephew, Menno, she seemed in great spirits. A lovely addition to our church district.

The youth had a volleyball game and snacks at our farm on Saturday before church. It was nice to have so many young people at the farm. They grow so fast. The boys were helpful in setting up for the event and I appreciated the young girls who helped clean up. Was barely any work for me at all.

Our own John is getting busy involved with his church instruction this summer and it appears that he will be taking his kneeling vow this fall. We are looking forward to his baptism just as we are looking forward to John David's wedding to Ella. I was surprised to see her name on the circle letter as I wasn't certain if the wedding was public knowledge yet. However, I can see that we will have a new sister to welcome to the family in just another two months.

Will be headed to Rachel's this Friday for a meeting of the sisters. Looking forward to a visiting day to catch up on everyone in person.

May God bless each of you.

Lovina, Harvey and the kinner

"Someone's here, Mamm!"

Benjamin stomped up the stairs that led to the porch, throwing the door open before racing inside. His face was flushed and his eyes bright.

"Catch your breath, please!" Anna said, laughing at the joy on her son's face.

He gulped some air and took a few breaths. "It's a big truck. A horse truck!"

Anna frowned and wiped her hands on her apron. "A what?"

"A big truck with horses in it!"

Horses? She wondered if it was someone who had lost his way. It was easy to do on the back roads, especially if the driver had made one wrong turn. It wouldn't be the first time that someone would pull into the driveway, seeking directions. "Let's have a look-see, ja?" She placed her hand atop Benjamin's head as she passed him, heading toward the door that he had just burst through.

Sure enough, as she stood on the porch, she saw a large truck stopping at the top of the lane by the barn. It was too large to pull any further around the bend so the driver shut the engine and opened the door of the truck.

"What in the world...?" she said softly, curious as to why the truck was there. The man didn't seem to pay any attention to Anna as he walked around to the back of the horse trailer and began to open the large, metal door.

"Hullo there!"

She heard Isaac before she saw him emerge from the barn. Immediately, she felt more comfortable walking down the porch stairs and across the grass toward the truck. She didn't need to turn around to know that she had several shadows behind her. The children kept their distance but their curiosity certainly wasn't going to keep them away from the excitement in the barnyard.

"What's this, Isaac?" she asked softly as she approached her husband.

"Can't say," he responded, just as puzzled as Anna was. He took off his straw hat and wiped the sweat from his brow. His hair was pressed against his head from where his hat had rested, the ends curling up. "Hullo there! You have the right address then?"

A large man wearing a red baseball hat poked his head around the back of the horse trailer. "The Fisher farm?"

Isaac slid his hat back onto his head and approached the man. "Ja, that's us but we didn't order no horse," he said lightly. "Think I'd remember that."

The man stepped down from the back of the trailer, a long, brown lead rope in his hand. At the other end of the rope was a large, brown horse that jumped down from the back of the truck. Its hooves clicked against the driveway as it followed the man who approach Isaac and Anna. "Then this here is your horse," he said and handed the rope to Isaac. "Just sign this paperwork," he added, thrusting a piece of crumpled yellow paper at him.

"I'll take that!"

The three of them turned their heads at the same time as Steve jogged around the back of the truck. He was smiling as he approached them and reached for the paper. There was something giddy about his expression that caused Anna to frown, trying to make sense of what she was seeing. Steve? Smiling? Buying a horse?

"*Danke*," he said as he scribbled his name on the paper and handed it back to the man.

"Anytime," the man said, shoving the paper into his front pocket and tipping his hat at Anna. "Good day then," he added and hurried back to the cab of his truck.

For a long moment, no one spoke as the man backed the truck out of the driveway. Steve stood there, holding the lead rope in one hand as he stroked the neck of the horse with another. When the truck finally disappeared, he glanced over at his brother and Anna.

"What in the world?" Anna asked, breaking the silence.

"It's a horse," Steve said simply.

She laughed. "Well, I can see that! But why on earth would you buy a horse?"

He gestured over his shoulder. "For my new buggy," he replied, as if it was the most obvious thing in the world.

Sure enough, around the backside of the barn, closer to the road, was a brand new black buggy with a grey top. The wheels and shafts were shiny black, having been freshly painted. Through the window, the navy blue seats could be seen. Indeed, it was a brand new buggy that must have arrived earlier that day for no one had seen it during the morning milking.

Without waiting for a response, Steve started walking toward the horse barn, leading the new horse past the gaping expressions of Isaac and Anna who stood there, mouths open, watching him. He didn't have to turn around to see that they glanced at each other before following him.

"Steve Fisher !" Anna started.

He ignored her but kept smiling as he led the horse into an empty stall.

The *kinner* were laughing quietly, standing behind their mamm who stared at their uncle, her hands on her hips. "I want to know what her name is!" Anna finally demanded.

"Anna!"

She looked at Isaac who was clearly horrified at his wife's blunt question. "It's obvious, isn't it? We can all tip-toe around wondering but I sure would like to know who I'm going to be welcoming into our family!"

Steve burst out laughed as he shut the stall door behind him. "Oh Anna," he teased. "Now I'm going to make certain you are the last to know!"

"I knew it!" Anna clapped her hands together in delight. "I just knew it! I prayed that it was true!"

He held up his hands in front of himself, still laughing. "But I'm not saying a word, Anna, not until I hear it from her directly," he said.

"I don't believe it!" Isaac said, joining in the laughter. "I suspected something was up but I didn't realize…"

"Now, now," Steve interrupted. "Let's not jump to conclusions too quickly."

"It's that glass girl who called, ain't so?"

Anna stared at her husband. "Glass girl?"

He waved his hand, trying to place the name. "The girl from Hostetler's Store."

Anna gasped. Of course. The young woman who had been at Leah's church service. The young woman who had paused and smiled at Steve when she poured his water. No wonder Steve had wanted to attend that church service at his sister's district when she was hosting it. "Mimi Hostetler?"

Isaac snapped his fingers. "That's her name," he said, pleased with himself. "She's a fine woman with a *wunderbaar* reputation. A right *gut* choice, Steve."

"You are all getting way ahead of yourselves," he

countered, trying to look serious. "Can't a feller just want his own buggy?"

"She's a lovely woman," Anna agreed. "I'm so happy for you."

Steve shook his head and walked past them. "Incorrigible," he mumbled.

Ignoring Steve, Anna turned to Isaac. "I wonder if I need to start planning for a November wedding? I didn't plant enough celery, that's for certain!"

"I heard that!"

He shook his head, trying to wipe the smile from his face. The teasing from his brother and Anna didn't bother him. In fact, it warmed his insides. He had never thought that he'd be in such a position. He had given up hope of ever settling down and getting married. But the reality was that he had finally found a woman that intrigued him enough to considering sharing the rest of his life with her. If only, he thought with a flutter of his heart, he was certain she felt the same way…

Mary Ruth finished folding the last of the clothes from the line when she saw the children walking down the lane toward the house. Melvin was practically racing, excited that it was Friday. Tomorrow would be the day that Katie came visiting the Millers and he had talked all week about how he would meet her there and help her groom that pony.

Setting the folded black pants onto the top of the basket of clothing, she smiled as she watched the two girls try to keep up with Melvin. It was impossible. His legs were much longer and he wasn't about to slow down in order to accompany them.

"What's the hurry?" she asked as Melvin bounded up the steps.

"It's the weekend!"

"Same amount of chores tomorrow as today," she reminded him. But she smiled at his enthusiasm and cheerfulness.

After seven weeks of being around the children, she had seen a remarkable improvement in their demeanor. While they still spoke about their mamm, often as if she would walk through the door at anytime, Mary Ruth could see that, indeed, they were adapting to their new life, one that didn't include their mother. It wasn't because they missed her any less. Nee, Mary Ruth realized. They were just accepting the fact that she was no longer with them.

With a big sigh, Mary Ruth glanced across the barnyard toward the fields. She could see Menno behind the mules as they pulled the cutter. It had taken him a while to mention that it was time to cut the hay again. Mary Ruth had been certain to send the children on a made-up errand so that they wouldn't be home when their father was cutting the field where their mamm had been killed.

She was looking forward to Sunday, a quiet day of church and no work. She needed a day to relax and reflect, that was for sure and certain. The routine of tending the Yoder *kinner* wasn't very taxing but she was also looking forward to the following week for the children would be returning to school and her life would start returning to normal.

In the meantime, she glanced up at the sky and realized that it was almost dinnertime. It didn't look like Menno was going to stop cutting hay so she decided she'd pack a basket and walk it out to him. Such hard work under the midday sun required a break and some food to replenish his energy. He'd certainly want to finish cutting that field by nightfall so that the hay had enough time to dry properly before baling. With no rain in the forecast, the weekend was going to cooperate with his plans.

"Girls," she said as they finally caught up to Melvin. "I have the table set for dinner but I think I'll take some food to your daed. He's awful busy and may not want to stop. Did your mamm have a basket? I'll take it to him after we eat, ja?"

Rachel sat before the doctor, trying to understand what he was saying to them. Small cell lung cancer. Spread to his bones and liver. Immediate need for treatment. Two months to live. The words sounded like a foreign language. She blinked as she stared at the balding man on the other side of the dark wood desk. He wore a black suit with a fancy tie and looked like he knew what he was saying. But the words didn't make sense to Rachel.

"I'm sorry," she interrupted him, leaning forward so she could hear better. "Are you reading the results for *my* husband? Elijah?"

The doctor paused, folding his hands on the single folder that was on the desk. Besides a tall desk lamp and three wooden photo frames, there was nothing else on the desk. "Yes, Mrs. Zook."

"Rachel," she prompted.

He took a sharp breath of air. "Rachel, these results are from the tests that we conducted on Elijah. The PETscan clearly showed that the growth has spread…"

"Elijah Zook?" she interrupted again, pointing to her husband who was silently seated next to her. "Lung cancer?"

Neither man spoke. They both stared at her, their silence telling her what she didn't want to hear.

"That's impossible," she said, dismissively. "He can't have lung cancer! He's Amish! He's never smoked. We don't smoke! Only people who smoke get lung cancer."

"Rachel," Elijah said gently, his voice shaking. "During my *rumschpringe*…"

"Oh nonsense," she scoffed. "That was years ago!"

"Mr. and Mrs. Zook," the doctor said softly. His expression was serious and indicated that this was not the first time that he had faced such opposition to horrific news. It was the part of his job that, clearly, he despised the most. "I can assure you that lung cancer is not always caused by smoking. Arguing over the how and the why isn't going to help at this point. It's a very fast moving cancer."

Silence.

"We don't have a lot of time," he stated.

Now that he had their attention, he began to explain the options. Once again, Rachel felt as if this man was speaking a foreign language. She didn't understand any of what he was saying. In fact, before a few hours ago, she had never known this man. Yet now she was forced to entrust her husband's life in his hands?

Menno stopped the mules and watched as Mary Ruth walked up the incline, the basket of food hooked over her arm. Her feet were bare and dirty, as was the bottom of her dress. She had been washing the floors before the children returned home. She wore a thin blue scarf on her head, not having wanted to soil her prayer kapp while she worked. Stray strands of brown hair clung to the back of her neck, which was as tan as her arms from working in the sun on Menno's garden.

She could feel his eyes on her, staring at her and, for just the briefest of moments, she felt uncomfortable. Why was he staring at her like that, she wondered. He hadn't paid her much attention at all since she had begun helping with the children, although he had offered to take her and Melvin over to the Miller's farm the previous weekend to meet up with Katie and Eleanor.

"Menno?" she asked, breaking his trance. "You feeling all right?"

He blinked once, still staring at her. The silence was awkward as was the expression on his face. She noticed that the color drained from his cheeks and his eyes, still so sad from remembering the loss of his wife, looked dull and lifeless. But the anger was gone from him and for that, she was thankful.

"Nee, nee," he said, quickly averting his eyes and shaking his head. "I'm sorry," he added quietly.

"For what?" she asked, lifting the basket and placing it on the side of the cutter.

"Staring," he admitted guiltily.

"Oh."

He glanced at the basket. For a moment, the mask of sadness lifted from his face. Holding the reins in one hand, he lifted the edge of the cloth that covered the food. She didn't have to look to know what he saw: fried chicken, coleslaw, and boiled potatoes with a thermos of meadow tea made fresh, just that morning. "*Danke*, Mary Ruth," he said.

"You're welcome," she responded. He looked at her again and, for the briefest of moments, she felt a flutter inside of her chest as if her heart had skipped a beat and her blood raced through her veins. She didn't like how he was staring at her and wondered what he was thinking. But then, she thought, it might be better to not know. There was nothing left to say so she turned, intending to head back to the house and away from those eyes.

"You reminded me of her just then."

His words stopped her feet from moving. It was the way his voice cracked when he said it. There was a clear sound of desperation in his tone, a sadness that she had never heard before that day. The realization hit her that, despite almost two months having passed, there was a depth of loss in this man's life. She couldn't begin to imagine what he felt and how hard he was struggling with healing.

"I'm sorry for your loss, Menno," was all that she could think to say. What else was there *to* say? "It's barely been two months, ja?"

"It feels like longer," he whispered.

She wasn't certain how to respond.

"I don't remember what she looks like," he said, lifting his eyes to meet hers once again. His blue eyes mirrored the sadness that was in his voice. "I had forgotten, you see. And I feel guilty about that."

"Menno…" She wanted to tell him that it was normal, memories were bound to fade. It was part of the healing process to move on with one's life and leave the past behind. However, she knew that thinking it and doing it were two very different ends of the spectrum. Without having walked in his shoes, she couldn't form the words to try to comfort him. It was a journey that he would have to take on his own.

"But just now," he said, his face lighting up for just a split second. "The way you looked…it reminded me of her."

Again, she remained silent. There was nothing to say in response to his words.

That moment of joy on his face disappeared and his shoulders sagged as he glanced across the field. Taking off his straw hat, he wiped the sweat from his brow with the back of his arm. He had done a lot of work so far that day but he had plenty more to do. He had been at work before she had arrived that morning. She knew from experience that it was hard, tiring work, the kind of work that made a body and soul weary.

"I can't do this alone," he said in a matter of fact tone.

She took a step toward him. "You have no choice," she said gently.

"I don't want to do this alone," he retorted.

She sighed. Alone. A terrible word. "You aren't alone. You have the *kinner*. They can help."

"You help."

She laughed despite herself. "I can't stay here forever!" She missed home and her mamm and Anna with her *kinner*. She wanted to enjoy some free time, time without caring for others and indulge in a little bit of time with someone caring for her. The comfort of home couldn't be replicated, that was something she had learned during the past weeks.

Menno took a deep breath and stared at her, silent for just a moment. If she wondered what was floating through his mind, she never would have imagined the words that he would speak next. She knew that he was lonely. She knew that he was missing his wife. No man should lose his soul mate in such a tragic manner and, even worse, at such a young age. But she also knew that she had to move on. Once the children were in school, she wanted to return home and to her own life, despite the fact that she could barely remember what her own life looked like.

He was staring at her again. The sadness had vanished from his eyes, replaced with something else that startled her. She couldn't place the emotion that she saw there. It was as if something had switched inside of him, something powerful strong...an idea that gave him hope.

"You can stay here," he said.

You can stay here. The words echoed in her head. She had to repeat them not certain that she had heard him properly. Stay there? At his farm? Whatever was he talking about?

"I'm sorry. I don't understand," she asked, frowning as she repeated, once again, the words that he had spoken: *You can stay here.* He was ferhoodled, dumbstruck with grief, she told herself and took a step backward. Her heart raced and she wondered if he had slipped over an edge into madness.

And then, he cleared his throat and said four words that nearly knocked her off of her feet.

"You can marry me."

This time, she didn't have to ask him to repeat his words. From the way that he was staring at her, she knew that she had heard him properly. There was a look of serenity and peace in his expression, as if his statement had made perfect sense and was completely logical. Perhaps it did...to him. But Mary Ruth couldn't stop her heart from beating inside of her chest. She was shocked at his offer, stunned into speechlessness. There were no words to express what she was feeling at that moment.

"Mary Ruth," he said quickly, wrapping the reins from the mules onto the side of the cutter so that they couldn't move. He jumped down and rushed toward her. "Yes, you can stay here but as my *fraa*," he said calmly, reaching out with a hesitant hand to touch her arm.

The feeling of his fingers on her skin caused her to jump. No one had ever touched her before, not like that. She moved away from him, staring into his face. *Has he lost his mind*, she asked herself. Clearly. "Menno, I..." she started to respond but the words wouldn't form on her lips. "You must have been in the sun too long," she said softly. She didn't want him to feel embarrassed yet she was having a hard time processing the fact that he appeared serious about what he had said. "You aren't thinking proper."

He shook his head. "Nee, you're wrong. I'm thinking just right, Mary Ruth," he stated firmly. There was a glow in his eye, one that spoke of the dawning of a new idea. "The *kinner* need a mamm, I need a *fraa*."

This time, she frowned, hurt at his words. "I'm not marrying anyone to fill a job opening!" The words came out harsher than she intended. But she was angry. For almost two months, she had been tossed into the lives of the Yoder family, dealing with his angry words and criticism. She had grown attached to the children, that was true, but to have such an insult from their father? It was too great a burden.

Menno shook his head, still holding her arm gently. "Don't take it that way, Mary Ruth. That's not exactly what I meant," he gushed. "I mean that we all need you. In time, you and I will grow fond of each other, I'm sure of that."

"Fond?" She yanked her arm free from his touch. "*Fond* of each other?" The word sounded so harmless yet tasted dirty when she repeated it. She had never been so insulted in her life and, to make matters worse, it was over a marriage proposal! She started to walk backwards down the hill, backing away from him. "You enjoy your dinner, Menno Yoder. And drink plenty of that tea. I think the sun has warped your sense of thinking today," she said then turned and hurried away from him, fighting the tears that threatened to fall from her eyes.

Lovina sat at the table, listening to Rachel as she talked about the cancer. Lovina had hired a driver to bring her to her sister's house. Lizzie, Sylvia, and Leah were there, too. The only one missing was Anna who had volunteered to stay at Leah's and keep the children occupied while the Fisher sisters' talked.

She had thought they were having a sister meeting, fellowship over a nice noon meal. But dinner was on the counter, including her homemade potato filling that she had baked that morning. No one was hungry anymore.

"Chemotherapy?"

The way that Lovina said it sounded even scarier. It was a big word, one that they didn't use in every day dialogue. And to have it associated with lung cancer was almost unheard of in their small community. Amish men simply did not get lung cancer for the simple reason that Amish men didn't smoke.

But the doctor had gone over the results and showed them the statistics. People who didn't smoke did get lung cancer. And Elijah Zook was one of them.

Rachel shut her eyes, wishing away the day. Everything felt surreal, as if it wasn't happening, not in her world. Perhaps, she thought, this is just a bad dream. But wishful thinking wouldn't make reality go away. She had to be strong and to face the future, both the immediate and the long-term. Denying the truth would not get her husband's cured.

"Elijah says that he won't do it," she said softly.

There was a collective gasp around the table.

"Without it, he'll die!" Leah exclaimed.

"Thank you for pointing out the obvious," Lizzie snapped. "Do you always have to be so direct?"

"Please stop," Rachel said, rubbing her forehead. "I can't hear you two bicker today."

"What about alternative treatments?" Lovina offered. "One of my neighbors is getting treatment from some man in New Mexico. He's mailing her herbs and oils."

Lizzie rolled her eyes. "That's powwow medicine, Lovina. We all know it don't work!"

"That's not true!" Lovina snapped back at her sister. "She's doing just fine."

Rachel slapped her hand on the side of the table. "That's not helping!" Her voice was loud and sharp, bringing silence back to the room. "I have a serious problem here, Lovina. Elijah has no energy and is not willing to do chemotherapy. This is serious, and powwow medicine is not the answer. Can you please, for once, stay focused?"

As always, Sylvia came to the rescue. She reached out her

hand and placed it over Rachel's. With a soft voice, she asked, "What will you do?"

A simple question with no simple answer. It was clear that, without treatment, Elijah would die. Rachel understood his reluctance to undergo chemotherapy. It was worldly medicine with a lot of negative side effects. But giving up wasn't the answer either. Somehow, Rachel thought, we have to convince him to get treatment.

"He needs to get treatment," she said in response to Sylvia. "Without it, he'll die and I can't do this on my own." She lowered her eyes, fighting the tears. "I can't do this without him," she whispered.

Katie ran through the Yoder's field. Anna had given her permission to visit the Miller's so that Katie could groom Butterscotch. As she approached the farmhouse, Katie slowed down, catching her breath. She wanted to stop into the Yoder's to see if Melvin wanted to walk over to the Miller's with her so that he could help with the grooming.

To her surprise, she found him standing on the front porch, staring at the field. The expression on his face was blank and Katie could tell that he was deep in thought.

"Melvin? You OK?"

He shook his head at the sound of her voice and turned to face her. "Katie Fisher . I'm surprised to see you here today," he said, his voice flat.

Standing at the bottom of the steps, she had to crane her neck to look up at him. "What's wrong?"

He shrugged and thrust his hands into his front pockets. "Ain't sure," he replied.

That didn't make sense to Katie one bit.

"Well, something had to happen to make you stand out here

and look so gloomy."

Again, he shrugged, but after a hesitation, he pointed over his shoulder. "It's Mary Ruth," he said. "She's crying."

She frowned. That also made no sense to her. Mary Ruth was one of the strongest people she knew and not prone to tears. In fact, Katie couldn't remember ever having seen Mary Ruth cry at all. "My aendi?"

"Ja," Melvin said, nodding his head once. "For about fifteen minutes or so."

Slowly, she climbed the steps. "Why?"

"Don't know," he said. "But I reckon my daed said something to her. Bet she stops coming here now. It'll be like losing my mamm all over again."

The thought horrified Katie. How could he possibly compare Mary Ruth's leaving to his own mamm's death? "Well, she has to come home at some point, ain't so?"

"I guess," Melvin agreed meekly. "Guess I just got used to her being around."

Katie glanced over his shoulder at the open door. "Did you ask her what's wrong?"

"*Nee*," he admitted.

"Well then," Katie said, lifting her hands in the air. "You can't be sure of anything, can you now? Let's go talk to her. Find out what's bothering her." Reaching for his hand, Katie started to lead him back into the house. "Come on, then," she insisted, pulling him along behind her.

Inside the house, Katie saw that Mary Ruth was seated at the table, her hands covering her face. The way that her shoulders shook, it was quite evident that she had, indeed, been crying. The thought shocked Katie and, slowly, she walked toward her aendi, curious and concerned as to what could have made Mary Ruth so upset.

"Mary Ruth?" she whispered. "What's wrong?"

Wiping at her eyes, Mary Ruth quickly stood up and turned her back to the two wide-eyed children. "Nothing, nothing," she lied. Then, as an afterthought, she added, "Nothing that concerns you, Katie."

"You're crying."

"What are you doing here, Katie?" Mary Ruth asked, changing the subject as she began to clean up the dishes from dinner. The children had eaten at noon, just before she had walked out to Menno and had that disturbing conversation.

"Mamm said I could go visit Butterscotch. Thought Melvin would like to come, too," she said.

Mary Ruth tried to force a smile. "That was right thoughtful of you, Katie."

Melvin shook his head. "I don't think I should go now, Katie. Mary Ruth shouldn't be alone," he whispered.

"Nonsense," Mary Ruth replied, taking a deep breath and trying to force the sadness from her heart. She wasn't certain why she was so bothered by what Menno had said. She understood why he had said that…why he had made the offer. She should feel honored but she didn't. Instead, she felt offended, insulted that what should be a joyous moment, the moment of a man proposing marriage, was a solution to a problem instead of love.

"He thinks you're going to leave," Katie said softly.

"Leave?" she repeated, staring at Melvin. "Why would I leave?"

He averted his eyes and stared at the floor. With his hands clasped behind his back and his expression so sad, Melvin resembled Menno and, in that moment, Mary Ruth felt her heart flutter. She realized something powerful important…she loved these children and leaving wasn't an option.

"I know my daed hasn't been himself since Mamm died,"

he said. "He's been hurtful toward you and I figured you were crying because of something he said." When he lifted his eyes, there were tears threatening to fall. "But that's not my *daed*, Mary Ruth. He's a right *gut* man with a large heart. He doesn't yell and he doesn't say mean things. Not my daed…at least not normally. He was awful *gut* to my mamm and to all of us…before she died."

You can marry me.

The insult stung less as she listened to Melvin. He was a sweet boy in great need of attention from his daed, much more so than love and hugs from her. And the little girls…they needed a mamm to brush their hair and teach them how to cook. But Mary Ruth knew that the last thing *she* needed was a husband, especially if that husband was Menno Yoder.

He had been rough with her, spoken to her in words that would have made most women cry long before today. She had learned how to stand up to him. By doing so, she had helped him begin the healing process. She had seen him through the worse, helped him accept the loss of Martha. Still, the memory of his angry eyes and booming voice still hurt her. He was the furthest man from her vision of a husband, not for her and not like this.

But the children…

"I'm not leaving," Mary Ruth said, her voice firm and strong. She reached her hand out to touch Melvin's shoulder and, when he fell into her arms, she gave him a warm hug. The strength of his arms around her waist and the warmth of his body touched her heart. And at that moment, she knew what she had to do. "I'm not going anywhere, Melvin. I promise you that."

Chapter 8: Ella's Letter

Dear Fisher Family,

What a gut surprise to find a package of letters awaiting me in my Mamm's mailbox. I am honored to have been included in the Fisher Family Circle Letters, despite not being a Fisher ...yet.

With autumn just around the corner and the fall baptism almost here, both John David and I are looking forward to November and our upcoming wedding.

We are also looking forward to establishing a home together. I pray that God leads us to a nice farm so that John David may continue farming, unlike so many others who have not been blessed with that option.

Mamm and I have been canning chow-chow and beets. We are looking forward to when the apples are ready for picking so that we can make applesauce. And Daed is taking a cow to butcher for canning meat. I will be certain to send some home with John David for everyone to enjoy.

My entire family continues to pray for Elijah, that the good Lord will care for him during his sickness.

May God bless all of you and your families.

Ella Yoder

It was late Thursday afternoon when Steve decided to pick

up Mimi at her work place and take her for a drive in the new buggy. It was unusual for him to leave the farm in the middle of the week, but he knew that he might not see her over the weekend. With a late season hay cutting scheduled at his daed's farm on Saturday and church on Sunday, he knew it would be a busy weekend.

Steve hadn't told Mimi about having purchased the horse and buggy. Instead, he had decided to surprise her. For the past few days, he had tried to imagine how she would react and if she would realize what his decision to stop using a driver for his errands truly meant.

When he pulled into the parking area of the store, Steve guided the horse to the side of the building. There were the hitching posts for the Amish drivers. He noticed that there were no cars in the lot nor were there any other buggies.

Once he climbed down from the buggy, he tied the horse to the hitching post, pausing to run his hand down the mare's sleek neck. He had spent a good part of the previous weekend with the horse, getting to know her and practicing driving her so that he could become familiar with her quirks and personality. After all, every horse had different ones, he reckoned.

For a moment, he smiled to himself, thinking back to his childhood and his daed's horse, Star. Throughout that horse's entire life, it would obstinately refuse to walk into water puddles, however small, but chose instead to either veer away at the last second or simply jump over them. Once Steve had gotten used to Star's quirky behavior, it hadn't been much of a deal, since Star was, otherwise, the perfect driving horse, but it had taken Steve a while to get used to it. In fact, he had even taken a liking to it, thinking of how it broke the monotony of his travels, way back when he first learned how to drive the horse as a teenager. He had even enjoyed witnessing the frightened reactions of the unaware girls he occasionally took to a singing or a volley ball game.

That had been so many years ago, he thought with a touch of nostalgia. Now that he was a man and looking toward the future, that kind of quirky behavior from his mare would not bode well with Mimi. He certainly did not want to take a chance on anything going wrong, that was for sure and certain.

The mare was a fast but honest horse with only one issue that he could identify: she knew her way back to the farm where she had come from and continually tried to return there. Twice during the past week, she had pulled herself free from the hitching post and started to slowly trot down the lane. Once, Steve had caught her on the road. The second time, the original owner bought her back, laughing about the homesick mare.

Steve knew that it would take time for the horse to learn that the Fisher farm was now home.

The hanging bell to the Hostetler's store rang when he opened the door. He shut the door behind himself and, taking a deep breath, walked down the narrow aisle toward the front counter. He could see her, bent over some papers and unaware that he was watching. She frowned, scribbling something in the margin of the yellow pad next to the files. Then, thinking twice about it, she erased it quickly.

"So serious," he said quietly, gently laughing when she jumped. Clearly he had startled her. "Sorry, Mimi," he apologized. "Didn't mean to scare you, now."

A broad smile warmed her face and he noticed that she reached up to brush a stray hair back under her prayer kapp. "I didn't hear you come in, Steve." She glanced around to see if anyone else was nearby. "I didn't know you were stopping in, either." A look of alarm crossed her face as she realized that it was a Thursday, not the typical day for a man to come calling. Since the family was so concerned about Elijah and his cancer, she immediately panicked that something bad had happened. "Is everything all right or did you just need to pick up something?"

"Ja," he said, leaning against the counter. "Everything is fine. Just needed to pick up something."

"Well, I'll be happy to get it for you," she replied, a smile of relief lighting up her face. "What did you need to get?"

"You."

The single word surprised her and she frowned for just a moment. At first, she didn't understand. But then, she laughed and reached out to touch his hand. "Me? I didn't realize I was store inventory, Steve Fisher !"

He laughed with her, delighting in the touch of her hand on his. Her comfort around him was charming and reassuring at the same time, a true blessing and indication that he was on the correct track. If he had always felt terribly uncomfortable around other women, he felt completely at ease around Mimi.

"Might you leave a bit early today?" he asked. "I want to show you something."

It took her but just a few minutes to locate her daed in the back storeroom and inform him that she was going to leave early, if he didn't mind. When her daed glanced up and saw Steve by the counter, he smiled and nodded. He raised his hand in greeting to Steve and gave a wink at Mimi. "See you at supper?"

She shrugged her shoulders. "Ain't sure," she replied casually, curious about Steve's unusual appearance at the store and knowing only too well that her daed was bursting at the seams with unspoken questions and hopes. "Steve wants to show me something."

Outside, Steve helped her into the shiny black buggy with the grey top. He noticed her glance at the plush blue seats as she touched the fabric. But she said nothing. He sat next to her and backed up the horse until they were able to turn and head down the road. The mare lifted her head, her mane fluttering in the air as she trotted gaily across the main road, free of an overcheck strap as

Steve didn't like to use them, considering them too restrictive.

He guided the mare down a side street then turned the buggy left at the next stop sign and headed toward the main street. But Mimi didn't speak. He glanced at her, wondering why she wasn't saying anything. Why didn't she ask about the obviously new buggy? Why didn't she comment about the gorgeous young horse that trotted so regally...so eagerly...down the street?

They rode in silence, each moment dragging longer and longer for Steve. In the past, he had always borrowed Isaac's or even John David's buggy. She had always teased him, commenting about his borrowed buggies. Now that he had finally taken that step in order to properly court her, she hadn't even noticed!

Silence.

When they turned down the road and crossed over Route 340, he glanced at her one last time. She was staring straight ahead, perfectly content as if she hadn't perceived anything different at all. But that moment gave him the opportunity to study her as the horse trotted down the road. She was truly a very pretty woman with such lively eyes and high cheekbones. Unlike other women, her skin was neither freckled nor tanned, probably because she spent so much time indoors at the store. He wondered how she felt about working outdoors, especially since she probably hadn't ever done much more than help in her mamm's garden.

"You awful quiet," he finally said.

A smile. "Guess the same could be said of you," she replied.

He held the reins in his hands, feeling the back and forth jiggle of the leather as the horse continued trotting at a steady pace. "You wondering anything?"

She kept staring straight ahead. "Not particularly."

He frowned. "Nothing?"

She shook her head. "Not really."

He was stunned. She was always so observant and quick to comment. This was a new side of Mimi that he had yet to experience. "You mean to tell me that you didn't notice anything?"

He saw her purse her lips as if trying to mask a smile. "Steve Fisher !" she finally said, turning to look at him straight on. "If you have something you want to say to me or show me, I suggest you just do it rather than try to get me to say it." Her eyes twinkled and she couldn't hide her delight. "But I'll just do it anyway since I can tell it's just tearing you up that I haven't noticed your fine new horse and fancy new buggy."

A gasp escaped his lips. She had known and hadn't said anything. She had been teasing him and he had fallen for it. Again. "Why! Aren't you the tricky one?" he whispered, his own eyes sparkling at her playfulness.

Laughing, she laid her hand on his arm. "Oh Steve! What made you do it?"

The fact that she asked that question concerned him. Hadn't she been so insistent on not courting in a buggy? Hadn't she teased him about constantly borrowing his brothers' or daed's buggies? Didn't she know the answer? "Well...I..." he stammered. "I thought..."

Noticing his discomfort, she stopped laughing and chewed on her lower lip. "You thought what, Steve?"

He cleared his throat and glanced at the road then back at her. "I thought you'd prefer courting in a buggy that wasn't borrowed," he finally blurted out, hoping that he hadn't presumed too much with Mimi. Perhaps she didn't feel as strongly about him as he did about her. His heart fluttered inside of his chest, knowing that if she said the wrong thing, it would break forever. Long ago, he had given up hope of finding a young woman who made him long for family life. But that had changed the day he had first walked into Hostetler's Store and laid eyes on Mimi.

"Steve," she started, the solemnness of her voice

frightening him.

"I shouldn't have presumed," he mumbled and started to turn the horse around, embarrassed at the way the conversation had shifted.

"What are you doing?" She sounded alarmed as they quickly started back up the road toward Route 340.

"Taking you home," he replied. "I made a mistake."

"Oh Steve," she sighed and sank back into the seat. "Stop the buggy for a minute. Please," she pleaded.

Reluctantly, he did as she requested but continued avoiding her eyes. How could he have misread her? How could he have thought that she might actually be interested in an old bachelor like him? He cringed waiting for her next words.

And then she said them. With softness in her voice that he had never heard before, she leaned forward and whispered, "Don't you realize that I would have courted you in a borrowed buggy, any buggy, even a car if that meant it was the only way to be near you!" Then, to his surprise, she lightly brushed her lips against his cheek. "I thought you knew that, by now."

He felt his heart race and he stared at her. His skin tingled where she had kissed him. It was the first time that a woman had kissed him and he was stunned at her sweet boldness. "Does that mean…?" The hesitation lingered between them and he couldn't form the words. "You mean that you might eventually consider to…" He paused, the words stuck in his throat. "You would one day…"

Finally, feeling sorry for him as he stumbled over his words, she said it for him. "If you are asking me to marry you, Steve Fisher ," she started, her eyes sparkling and a hint of a smile on her lips. "The answer has been and certainly is a very happy yes! I just wonder what took you so long to ask!"

A very happy yes.

His ears seemed to ring and he couldn't digest what it was that he had just heard. He hadn't intended to propose to her. Not today. Not like this. It had only been a few short months of courting. But he had known that he would ask her and he now knew that, with Mimi Hostetler, no planning was necessary because nothing ever went as planned.

A very happy yes.

"I...I don't know what to say." This day certainly wasn't going the way he had planned it. "I'm speechless," he said in complete disbelief. He had wanted to find out if she cared about him in the same way he cared about her. Instead, they were engaged!

"Is that a happy speechless?" she teased.

"Ja!" he said, slowly allowing a smile to cross his face. The realization hit him that Mimi Hostetler had just agreed to be his bride. Beautiful, fun, and playful Mimi Hostetler had just said yes and committed to spend the rest of her life with him. They would move to his farm, work side-by-side, hopefully have children, and worship God together. Mimi Hostetler was his soul-mate, the very one that he had been waiting for all of his life, despite not knowing it. God had a plan for him, after all.

"A very happy speechless," he said and reached over to hug her, his arms wrapping her in an embrace that he vowed would never end.

It was Friday. Mary Ruth had just finished making some fresh bread for the Yoder children to enjoy when they would return home from school. Her life had taken a pleasant turn into a new routine, now that school had started. She would spend the mornings helping her sister, Leah, and then head to the Yoder farm after dinner. That gave her time to do afternoon chores and prepare the supper meal.

Still, despite the simpler routine, something had been eating at her. She found herself not able to concentrate or focus. For three weeks, she had been tossing and turning at night, thinking back to that strange proposal from Menno Yoder in the hayfield. She thought about Melvin's concern that she would leave and how he was so afraid that he'd lose her, too. She thought about how much she had come to love those children.

Just that morning, Mary Ruth's mind had been in a complete whirl. She was so distracted that Leah had asked her three times what was wrong. When Mary Ruth had hung up the laundry, she hung up the dirty clothes and started re-washing the clean. Leah finally told her to go lie down for clearly she was ferhoodled beyond being of any help.

But that didn't help.

Fortunately, during the past three weeks since that uncomfortable discussion with Menno in the hayfield, she had been able to avoid him. It hadn't been too hard since the children had returned to school and now Mary Ruth only came in the afternoons to clean the house, wash the clothes, and prepare supper. During that time, Menno was usually busy with his chores in the dairy barn or in the fields. Yes, avoiding him in person had been easy, she thought.

Except for one time.

She had just finished straightening the upstairs when she heard the door open. The hinge was rusty and squeaked. She was shutting the door to Melvin's bedroom, her arms carrying his dirty pants and some shirts, when she heard the downstairs door slam shut. She knew it was too early for the children to be home so that it meant Menno had come into the house. Taking a deep breath, she started walking down the stairs, holding the railing with one hand. She paused at the end of the staircase and looked around the kitchen. No one was there. Perhaps, she had wondered, I imagined the door?

Setting Melvin's dirty clothes on the edge of the kitchen table, she had walked over to collect the dishtowels from the counter. She had already brought down the girls' clothing and, with everything gathered together, she headed into the washroom, her arms full of laundry. It was when she had started the washtub, the warm water flowing into the big basin, that she felt as if she was no longer alone. Her back stiffened and she turned her head, glancing over her shoulder.

He has been standing in the doorway, watching her. It was the first time that they had seen each other these past two weeks and she didn't know what to say. Studying his expression, she tried to get a reading on his mood. His blue eyes were no longer dull and lifeless. Instead, there was a new look, one of curiosity and interest.

Neither one of them spoke.

Instead, he had simply tipped his head at her as a way of extending a silent greeting before he had hurried out the side door to return to the barn.

Shutting off the water, Mary Ruth had dried her hands on her apron and walked over to the screen door. He was walking back to the barn, his hands in his pockets and his broad shoulders dipped down. With a frown, she had returned to the chore of washing the clothes. It was later, when she walked back into the kitchen, that she had found the flowers in a glass, half filled with water, on the table. Her heart fluttered and she had glanced out the kitchen window. Had he left those flowers for her?

That had been earlier in the week. And she hadn't been able to stop thinking about the look in his eyes when he had stared at her. She couldn't stop wondering why he would have left those flowers.

Now, as she stood at the counter, her hands covered in flour and the kitchen not as tidy as she would have liked it, she thought back about those flowers. Her stomach jumped and she bit her lower lip, wondering why he had left them on the table. It was a far cry from the weeks that he had spent yelling and ranting at her. Of course, he had softened a bit in recent weeks and then came his offer. Since then, He hadn't spoken to her, hadn't apologized for his strange behavior. But clearly it was a gesture. She just didn't know what to make of it.

"Mary Ruth."

She spun around, startled out of her deep thoughts at the sound of his voice. Backing against the counter, she lifted her hand to her chest and tried to catch her breath.

He was standing by the table. She hadn't heard him enter the room. He must have oiled that hinge, she thought. Even more strange was the fact that he was dressed in his Sunday clothing, his hat in his hand. For a moment, he seemed to be nervous as he stared at her, that same look of curiosity in his face that she had noticed on the day of the flower incident.

"I wanted to ask you to share a glass of ice tea with me on the porch," he said, his voice soft and low.

"Ice tea?"

He reached out his hand toward her. "Please," he pleaded.

Wiping her hands on her apron, she frowned. What on earth, she thought. "Well, reckon I should pour you a glass, then." She glanced at the counter. The bread could wait; it only needed a bit more kneading. "I made some fresh meadow tea yesterday," she said, hurrying to the refrigerator to take it out. He was still standing there, waiting and watching as she took two clean glasses down from the cabinet and poured the cold, fragrant tea into them.

He held the door open for her and she slipped by him. To her surprise, there was another bouquet of flowers already on the porch bench. This one was bigger than the previous flowers that he had left on the table for her. Carefully, she moved them and sat down, making certain that she was far enough away from Menno that her leg didn't brush against his.

For a few minutes, they sat there in silence. The birds were chirping from the dogwood tree by the corner of the house. In the field, the cows were wandering through the pasture, calling out to each other from time to time. The sky was perfectly blue and the air just right for early September.

"I wanted to talk to you," he finally said after he cleared his throat. "'Bout the other day in the hayfield."

"No need to apologize," she said quickly. "I understand your distress, Menno." She just wanted to get back into the kitchen, away from him and his overpowering presence. He was trying and she recognized that. Still, her own feelings were jumbled inside of her and she couldn't help but want to just run away.

But he had more surprises for her.

"I wasn't going to apologize," he said.

She frowned and looked at him. "Why ever not?"

That sparkle in his eye grew deeper and she realized that there was a hint of a smile on his lips. She hadn't seen him smile too often and it made him appear much younger. "Because I meant it," he said. "I meant what I said to you."

Oh help, she thought.

"Mayhaps I didn't go about it the right way," he admitted, his eyes scanning the fields for a moment. "But I meant what I said to you, Mary Ruth."

Her heart raced and she felt her palms begin to sweat. She didn't have to look into a mirror to know that her neck was bright red and the color was traveling up her cheeks. "Menno..." she began softly. "You're still grieving."

"I have a promise for you, Mary Ruth," he said, ignoring her. His hands fiddled with the glass and he stopped staring at the field. Instead, he made certain to maintain constant eye contact with her. "You stay here and you marry me. Be a *fraa* for me and mother for my *kinner*," he started. "And I promise that I will always be a right *gut* man to you. I will take *gut* care of you and work very hard to prove myself worthy of you so that, one day, I have your love."

Stay here and marry me.

She stared at him, repeating his words to herself. She didn't know this man and she certainly didn't love him. However, she knew that she loved his children. From what she had heard from everyone, he *was* a godly man and had been most kind to his wife, Martha. Now, as he stared at her with crystal blue eyes full of hope, she wondered why he had chosen her. Marriage was forever. She was not a replacement wife.

This isn't how it's supposed to happen, she wanted to shout. There was supposed to be a courtship and shy buggy rides. In her mind there were stolen glances at church service and whispers when no one was looking. But not once, in any of her dreams about finding a man to love, was there a previous wife who had just been killed in a farming accident that left the family grieving.

"Menno, I don't know what to say," she said, her voice soft and even. "It's a very flattering offer but I…"

"I will make you very happy," he said, interrupting her. "I will work hard every day to win your heart." He took a deep breath. "I know you are not Martha and she is never coming back. But you are Mary Ruth and I see God's blessing working through you."

If her heart would beat any faster, she was afraid that it would jump out of her chest. Her head felt dizzy and she wanted to run away. This isn't happening, she told herself. This isn't real.

But it was real.

"Menno," she said slowly, avoiding his eyes. She didn't

want to see the hope that was there. "I really think I need to finish that bread." She didn't wait for his response but quickly stood up and, without another word, she started to open the door.

"Mary Ruth!"

She turned around and, despite herself, she looked at him.

He stood up and held his hat in his hands again. There was a look of humility about him but also a look of peace. "You saved me and I want to spend the rest of my life thanking you for that. Real actions, not just words, to show you how much I care about you and for what you have done for me and my *kinner*." He slid his hat on his head and gave her a small smile. "You think on that, ja?" This time, it was Menno who didn't wait for a response but turned around and walked down the steps of the porch and headed toward the barn.

She stood there, her hand on the door and one foot inside of the house. His house, she realized. Her eyes watched him as he walked away, taking in his broad shoulders and confident walk. There was something about him that had changed and she realized that, indeed, he was saved. With a heavy heart, she walked through the doorway, determined to finish her chores and get home as fast as she could. She needed space and time to digest what he said and why her own heart had fluttered when he had smiled at her.

On Saturday morning, Katie sat at the kitchen table, helping her mamm make cookies. With church to be held the following day at a neighbor's farm, Anna had been selected to bring some desserts. Katie had offered to help with the cookies, an easy enough job and one that she particularly enjoyed since it meant she was able to eat little pieces of the dough when her mamm wasn't looking. While Katie plopped the sugar cookie dough onto the baking sheets, her mamm was making shoofly pies. Ella had stopped over to help and was bustling with good news.

"John David thinks he found a farm," she gushed, her eyes sparkling and her cheeks pink with excitement. "And it's just down the road!"

Anna gasped at the good news. It was hard to find farms in the area and many young couples had to move far away or accept jobs outside of farming if they wanted to stay in Lancaster County. "You don't say!"

"Um hum!" Ella nodded, happily working the dough into a pie pan while Anna prepared the pie filling. "He just took a day off to be down there yesterday. It's at the end of the lane and quite a fine farm. The older couple won't be moving until March... moving into the *grossdaadihaus* with their younger children in New Pequea. But they just can't handle the farm alone anymore."

Katie listened as Ella described the farmhouse and it's twenty acres. While small by most farm standards, Ella said she didn't mind. It was the perfect size to get started and would allow John David to keep helping his daed, Isaac, and Steve with their own farm work.

As the talk shifted to a spring garden and crops, Katie's mind wandered. She thought about Melvin and wondered if she would see him later that day. Her *onkel*, Steve, had volunteered to drive her over to the Miller's farm to take care of her pony that afternoon. But everyone suspected that the invitation had a hidden purpose: he wanted to sneak in a visit with Mimi after helping with the haying.

The door to the *grossdaadihaus* opened and Miriam walked inside. She was carrying a box, which she set on the table. "Katie," she said to her granddaughter. "Ask Steve if he'll drop this off for Rachel. I promised her some of my chow-chow. It's Elijah's favorite."

Ella laughed. "Not the same chow-chow recipe that you gave to me this summer?

Miriam turned to look at her future daughter-in-law, a

questioning look in her expression as she pondered Ella's question. Then, as if in a moment of clarity, she nodded and smiled. "Ach, ja! I reckon it is!"

With a twinkle in her eyes, Ella gestured toward a box on the table. "I bought some myself to give to the family! John David loves it so and I wanted to thank you for sharing the recipe with me!"

With a friendly clucking of her tongue, Miriam shook her head. "Well, don't that beat all!"

Wiping her hands on a towel, Anna hurried over to the box and pulled out one of Ella's jars of canned beans. The pretty colors of green beans, kidney beans, corn, and lima beans looked fresh and packed just perfect in the glass jar. She handed it to Miriam and teased, "Let's send that along and see how it compares!"

"Oh Anna!" Ella laughed and the other ladies joined in. "I'm more than certain I could never do as good a job as Miriam."

Tucking the Ella's jar into the box, Miriam sighed. "I'm sure they will both appreciate the gesture. Especially Elijah." Her eyes looked tired and there were dark circles under her eyes. She tried to smile at Katie as she said, "I want you to give Rachel this letter." Miriam tucked a small white envelope into the box. "Can you remember that?"

Katie nodded.

Ella looked up. "How is Elijah doing, Miriam? Has he made a decision yet?"

"*Nee*," Miriam said. "Rachel is still praying that he changes his mind." She paused. "We all are, I reckon."

"What's wrong with Elijah?" Katie asked.

Anna glanced at her daughter. Clearly Anna didn't want to discuss Elijah's health situation in front of her daughter. The last thing she wanted was to scare her, to have Katie wonder about the possibility that their own daed could fall ill. There was no reason to cause the children alarm. "Could you run out to see when the hay cutting will be over? Steve should get going soon if you're to have time with that pony before he brings you back home. And the others will have to start the late afternoon milking soon anyway. And check that the other *kinner* are not bothering your daed."

"But...?"

Anna put her hands on her hips and gave her daughter a stern look. "Now, Katie!"

For a moment, Katie stared at her mamm, wanting to ask more about Elijah. The way her mamm was chasing her outside clearly meant that something was happening. She didn't know why her mamm was sending her out of the house, but knowing that she had to be respectful, Katie obeyed and left the kitchen. After all, if she got in trouble with her mamm, there might be no visit to the Miller's Farm to see Butterscotch.

The church service was held at the Miller farm that Sunday. Even though the farm was old, the house had a typical room separated from the kitchen with a folding door. On church Sunday, the door would be folded back and between that room and the kitchen, the congregation would gather to worship.

No one ever complained about the close quarters. It was a time to join together, to sing praises to the Lord, and to cleanse the mind and soul for the upcoming week. That was how Mary Ruth looked at it. She often found herself reflecting on her own words and actions, finding fault with herself and praying for forgiveness and strength.

As usual, Mary Ruth sat with the other young, unmarried women and listened to the words of the hymn being sung by the congregation.

If we would be like Christ,
We must at all times
Love one another on earth,
Yes, not only with the tongue,
But with true deeds,
As John writes.
Those who only love with words,
Behold where love dwells.[3]

She stopped singing as the rest of the people continued with the next verse. In her head, Mary Ruth repeated the hymn. God wanted His people to not just speak the Word but to live the Word. Wasn't that something Menno had promised to her? That he wanted to show her with actions, not words, how much he appreciated what she had done? How she had saved him?

Love one another on earth. Her heart pounded as if the words had been sung just for her. God had a plan for His people and sometimes it wasn't the plan that the people expected. God didn't want people to love sparingly but completely. *At all times.* Who was she to question His plan for her?

Stunned with the realization, Mary Ruth looked around the room. On the opposite side, the men were seated on benches facing the center of the room. Her eyes scanned their faces until they fell on Menno. He was staring at the bishop, unaware that he was being observed from the other side of the room.

Melvin was seated next to Menno and the three little girls sat on the other side. At one point, Menno looked down at his *dochder*, Suzanna, and gave her an encouraging smile. He seemed to point to something in his hand and Mary Ruth realized that he was pointing to the location of the verse in the Ausbund. The young girl must have lost her way in the song and was trying to

---

[3] Ausbund Song 119 verse 12

find the word in the line. There was a kindness in his gesture, one that caught her off guard. *Actions, not just words*, she repeated the lesson from the hymn.

As the little girl returned her attention to the chunky book that Menno was holding, Menno took the opportunity to glance up and his eyes scanned the room. At that moment, he caught sight of Mary Ruth watching him. He kept singing but tilted his head slightly, both surprised and curious at her attention.

Quickly, she looked away, her cheeks flooding with color.

After the service, Mary Ruth set about helping the women prepare the serving platters of food. The men quickly transformed the hard wooden benches into tables and the children ran outside, enjoying the beautiful September day. With the sun shining and the air crisp, it was the perfect day for playing tag and swinging on the swings in the Miller's backyard.

Melvin wandered into the barn to visit with Butterscotch. Just the day before, Katie had insisted that he'd come with her to groom and ride the pony. They had taken turns, laughing as Butterscotch ran through the pasture when they climbed on the pony's back, their fingers holding her mane and their legs dangling by her side.

Leaning his head against the side of the stall door, Melvin watched the pony grazing on some hay. There would be no grooming on Sunday, lest he get an earful from the bishop. Truth be told, he would never dare to consider doing anything to the pony if Katie wasn't around, too. After all, he reasoned, it was *her* pony.

Still, he enjoyed being near Butterscotch. He could hear Katie's voice, giving him instructions and telling him the proper way to handle the pony. She was very good at taking charge and he liked that about her. He didn't have to think, to wonder, just follow her instructions. If only she lived close by, he thought, not for the first time. Quite often, he found himself waiting all week for her visits, anticipating the funny stories she would tell him or the adventures they would go on, taking turns riding Butterscotch and trotting through the fields.

"What are you doing in here, Melvin?"

He was surprised to see Mary Ruth walk through the door. In her black dress with freshly starched white apron and bib, she looked more stern than usual. He had grown used to her smile when he ran in from the barn or came home from school. He enjoyed his talks with Mary Ruth almost as much as he enjoyed listening to Katie.

"Thinking," he responded.

She leaned against the stall door. "About?"

He sighed and glanced at her. There was a grave hesitation in his voice. Rather than answer her question, he had one of his own. "Can I tell you something?"

The serious tone of his voice struck her. Whatever could be wearing so heavily on his mind? "Of course, Melvin," she said.

"Do you think it's possible to meet someone and know that they are the one for you at my age?" He looked away, trying not to look directly into her eyes. "I mean…well…I know love comes with time and all but I sure do get on well with Katie."

Mary Ruth sighed. "Oh Melvin," she said gently. "You have so much time ahead of you."

"But it happens, right?" He plucked at a loose piece of wood on the stall door. He stared at the pony and his eyes glazed over. "We sure do have fun on Saturdays when she can come out here to take care of Butterscotch. She is awful smart about horses, Mary Ruth. And I can talk to her." He looked at Mary Ruth. "Really talk to her. She understands how I feel about my mamm passing and all. She knows me in a way that others sure don't. I'd say that she's as *gut* a friend to me as any of the boys at school."

"Friends are special, indeed," Mary Ruth said gently.

He frowned, apparently not feeling as if Mary Ruth truly understood him. Taking a deep breath, he stared at her, his eyes strong and bright. "I mean, if we grow up as friends and all, that would be a right *gut* way, I think. But does it ever happen that friends at our age actually become more than friends at a later age?"

She didn't know how to respond. She had thought she would know when she met her soul mate, the one that God had chosen for her. At one point in time, she had envisioned long buggy rides and picnics by the river. She had envisioned little notes slipped into her hand at church Sunday or small pebbles tossed at her bedroom window late at night on a Friday.

It had never happened for her. Not yet, anyway.

On the other hand, it had happened that way for Rachel. Elijah had been her soul mate. He had taken her home from singings, driving the horse and buggy the long way in order to spend more time with Rachel. He had tossed small pebbles at her windows at night to visit with her when the rest of the family was sleeping. They had taken the kneeling vow together and announced their engagement shortly thereafter. After so many wonderful years together, now they were faced with the very strong reality that forever would only be a few more months.

So yes, Mary Ruth thought, it can happen. But just because it does, it doesn't mean its going to work out in the way envisioned.

"I've heard of such things, ja," she admitted slowly, not wanting to upset or discourage Melvin. "But it doesn't always happen the way we have it planned in our minds." Placing a hand on his shoulder, she smiled gently. "Time will tell if friendship can grow into love. But it's a right *gut* start to be friends, Melvin."

Content with that, he nodded.

"Now, come into the barn. I have some food set aside for you. The women are almost ready to clean the dishes and I don't want you to go hungry now," she said tenderly.

Side by side, they walked back to the large room in the house where the fellowship meal was being served. To her surprise, she saw a figure standing on the porch by the door. It was Menno and he stood by himself. He was watching the two of them as they walked closer. With his eyes upon her, never once flickering, Mary Ruth felt her heart begin to race and she wished, oh how she wished, that he wasn't there. The confusion and distress came rushing back to her after she had tried so hard to push them out of her mind.

"Son," Menno said as they approached the porch step. "You need some food, ja?"

Melvin nodded. "Mary Ruth saved me a plate."

"Go on in and eat then," he replied. "One of the women will help you find it."

Mary Ruth moved to follow Melvin, but as they walked by, Menno reached out and touched Mary Ruth's shoulder. She felt something in her blood and that too familiar flutter in her chest returned. Despite not wanting to, Mary Ruth paused and Menno looked her in the eye. She felt something slip into her hand and she frowned, looking down to see what it was. A folded piece of white paper. He looked flustered and nervous and started to walk away. But Mary Ruth didn't move. Instead, she opened the paper and read the words on it.

And she caught her breath.

He paused, looking over his shoulder at her, silently reading his note.

Her head was dipped own and she was staring at the paper.

Mary Ruth,
Complete my joy by being of the same mind, having
the same love, being in full accord and of one

mind[4].

Menno

She shut her eyes, her back to him. *Complete my joy*, he had written. Quickly, she turned around to face him, her eyes wide and frightened. He watched her, curious for her reaction. Neither one spoke, the silence hanging between them as if in an unspoken conversation.

And then she said it.

"Yes, Menno," she heard herself say, shocked at the words that rolled off of her tongue. She had no idea where they came from and, despite telling herself to stop, to refrain from responding, she heard five words slip from her lips; words that surprised both of them, equally: "I will complete your joy." She hesitated and pressed the piece of paper to her chest. Lifting her eyes to meet his, she whispered, "Yes, I will marry you."

---

[4] Philippians 2:2

Chapter 9: Mary Ruth's Letter

Dear Family,

I know my name is not on the circle letter list but I wanted to add my own letter to the package. I have something important to share with everyone.

Menno Yoder has asked me to marry him and I have agreed. This was not expected but I find that I am increasingly excited about being able to positively impact the lives of Melvin and his sisters.

May God bless all of you and your families.

Mary Ruth

Mary Ruth stared at the piece of paper, her words so carefully and neatly written staring back at her. *Decided to marry Menno Yoder!* When she read the words she sensed both a warm thrill and a shiver of fright travel up her spine. Her words were cold, direct and to the point. Just like Menno himself, she thought. A hint of the unknown that teased of mystery. By all accounts, it had been an unconventional courtship, if one could even call it that. She was still having a hard time embracing it.

Two weeks had passed since she had agreed to marry Menno. Since then, nothing had changed. She rarely saw him when she was at the house. She'd walk down the lane from Leah's in the afternoon as she always did, her eyes scanning the horizon for some sign of Menno. It surprised her that she was hoping that he might spend some time alone with her, courting her proper.

He didn't.

Yet, on more than one occasion, she had found flowers waiting for her on the table or a folded piece of paper with her name on it by the sink. She would open the note and read the Bible verse he had written for her, his penmanship surprisingly elegant and careful. His words touched her heart and she would walk outside, standing on the porch and look across the fields to see if he was out there, perhaps waiting to catch a glimpse of her searching for him.

He wasn't.

His avoidance of her conflicted greatly with his small gifts that let her know he was thinking about her.

Despite the turmoil of emotions that she felt, she never once doubted her decision. There was something about Menno Yoder that spoke directly to her soul. If only she knew for certain that he had some feelings for her and was not simply looking for a replacement wife!

With a sigh, Mary Ruth leaned her head against her hand and shut her eyes. A letter, she thought. I can't tell them in a letter! She could only imagine her mamm's reaction. Mamm would be shocked, that would be for sure and certain. Mary Ruth settling down into a ready-made family? There would be more than one shocked person in her own church district as well as in Menno's.

Crumpling up the piece of paper, she threw it into the garbage can, angry when it missed and bounced across the floor.

Church Sunday was the baptism of the new church members. It was especially crowded as more family members tried to fit into the room over at the Beiler's barn for this very special occasion. Mary Ruth sat at her usual place with the other unmarried women and realized that, within the next month or so, she'd be sitting with the married ones and, most likely, with Menno's children beside her. She'd be their *mamm* and it would be her responsibility to raise them according to the Ordnung and their father's beliefs. It bothered her that she hadn't more insight into his expectations of what, exactly, her role would be when it came to the *kinner*.

A sigh escaped her as she glanced around the room. She watched the youths kneel before the congregation and listened to their vows being spoken. It was only two years ago when she had taken her own kneeling vow. Time sure did seem to fly by since that day, she realized. After two short years, she had turned from an adolescent into the young, responsible woman she now was; and she was soon to be married!

She could remember how emotional she had been on that day. She fought tears several times, feeling overwhelmed with the decision that she was making. It was a commitment to her family, the community, the church, and –more importantly- to God. She hadn't wanted to disappoint anyone, especially her family and certainly not God.

Her eyes traveled to the section of benches where the married men sat. Despite being a widower, Menno had not changed where he sat during service. Nor would it change after they were married. *Seems like I'm the only one facing change*, she thought with a mixture of bitterness and sorrow.

At that moment, Menno noticed her watching him. His blue eyes met hers and he gave her a small smile. It was a reassuring look and she felt an electric shock run throughout her body. It was fast but it was strong enough to make her blush. Realizing that, she tried to look away but her cheeks deepened in color. She could feel the heat creeping down her neck, too.

Menno's lips twitched as though suppressing a bigger smile. Not only had he seen her blush but he knew exactly why.

Embarrassed, she excused herself and hurried down the stairs to the small bathroom located on the first floor of the building. She shut the door and the battery-operated motion light turned on, casting a dim glow throughout the room. She leaned against the door, her eyes shut and her heart pounding. How could she face him again, she thought to herself. He had seen her reaction to his gaze and knew that she blushed for him.

Calm down, she told herself. *It's natural!* But the truth was that she didn't know whether or not it was natural. She had never courted before and certainly had never committed to be a man's wife. And she had never felt the way she did when Menno had just looked at her.

Taking deep breaths, she moved toward the sink and turned the knob for cold water. She cupped her hands under the steady stream and splashed some water on her cheeks. The coolness helped her focus and concentrate on calming herself so that she could return to the church service before her absence was noticed.

The door creaked as she opened it and stepped outside. She shut the door as quietly as she could, hoping that the noise didn't carry upstairs.

To her surprise, Menno was leaning against the wall on the other side of the door. He was waiting for her, his hands thrust into his pockets and one foot crossed over the other. When she jumped back, he pushed off from the wall and approached her.

"You are ill, Mary Ruth?" he asked, concern in his eyes.

"*Nee,*" she said quickly but looked away.

He pulled a white handkerchief from his pocket and reached forward, gently dabbing some water droplets from her neck. "I saw you rush out of the service," he said, his voice low so that it wouldn't carry upstairs. "I was worried."

He was worried, she said to herself, feeling that thrilling wave of electricity again. *He cares!* "I just needed some air," she offered as an excuse. "You…you are well?"

"Ja, that I am," he replied and smiled gently. "I have to talk to the bishop this week about announcing our intentions at the next service. So I am quite well, Mary Ruth."

"I…" She paused, uncertain to how he would react if she

asked him the question that was soaring through her mind every minute of every day for the past two weeks. Yet, she didn't want him thinking that she was too forward.

The smile never left his lips. "You what?"

"I…I haven't seen you in almost two weeks, Menno," she whispered. "I'd have thought you changed your mind if I hadn't found the notes and flowers."

Immediately, the smile left his face but not due to anger or disappointment in what she said. Instead, it was a look of concern. "I was giving you space, Mary Ruth," he explained. "I know you are nervous about this decision and that you are the one giving up the most. I felt it best to not…" He hesitated as if searching for the appropriate word. "To not crowd you."

"To not crowd me?"

Now it was Menno's turn to look sheepish. "If I suddenly demanded all of your time, I was afraid *you* would have second thoughts, being that we haven't truly courted very much."

She raised an eyebrow. "We haven't courted *at all*, Menno."

"Ja, vell…" He scratched at his beard. "Reckon that's true."

Now! she told herself. Now was her chance to offer her suggestion to Menno. Her chance to let him know that she wanted to spend more time with him. "It…it might be nice to spend some time together, ain't so?" she offered shyly. She wasn't used to feeling so timid in front of anyone. "Mayhaps it might make us both feel a little better."

He stared at her, his blue eyes taking in the hopeful look on her face. The difference in their age was suddenly more apparent to him. He had presumed that she preferred having some space and not feeling crowded. An older woman would have felt that way, he thought. But the young woman standing before him, the woman he had committed to marry, was looking at him with the eyes of one who wanted courting and time to get to know him.

He hadn't been prepared for that.

Still, he knew that she was right. If they did spend some time together, did get to know each other, they both would feel more comfortable, indeed.

"Then I guess I best be giving you a ride home after service, now," he stated, his mind made up at once that, if courting was what she wanted, courting was what she would get. "I'll signal you when I'm ready to leave with the *kinner*." He forced an awkward smile at her then nodded toward the stairs. "Best go back now before tongues wag. There'll be time enough for that " He stepped back, indicating that she should pass him and walk up the stairs first. The gesture and the look on his face made her want to blush all over again. He was certainly holding up his end of the bargain.

It was after the fellowship meal when Leah and Rachel joined Mary Ruth as they helped wash the dishes. Mary Ruth smiled her appreciation at her sisters, but in doing so, saw Rachel up close for the first time that day.

"Sister!" she gasped. "Are you all right?"

Rachel clenched her jaw and reached for the towel on the counter. "I'd rather not discuss it," she snapped.

Mary Ruth glanced at Leah who merely shrugged and mouthed the word "Elijah".

Pursing her lips, Mary Ruth glanced around to make certain no one could hear her as she leaned over to her older sister. "You need to tell him that he must do the treatment!" she hissed. "This is not what God wants!"

"But," Rachel retorted in a similar tone. "It is what *Elijah* wants!"

"I don't understand!"

With a shake of her head, Rachel turned her attention back to the dishes. "Even with treatment, Mary Ruth, the disease is most likely terminal. He'd rather spend what time he has left here with us and do what he can to prepare for the end. God is going to call him home and there is very little we can do about it." She rubbed the plate in her hands. "I've seen how fast he is declining already. He's short of breath, coughs all of the time, and gets winded just walking up the stairs. It's progressing fast." She glanced up and stared at her two sisters, as if daring either of them to comment. "Too fast!" Slamming the towel down on the counter, she thrust the plate at Leah and turned on her heel. Quickly, before anyone could see the tears in her eyes, she hurried away.

Leah rolled her eyes. "That's great, Mary Ruth."

Mary Ruth glared at her. "What's that supposed to mean, Leah?"

Her sister merely shook her head. "You wouldn't understand. You aren't married," she responded and hurried after Rachel, leaving Mary Ruth standing at the sink with her cheeks turning bright red and her mouth hanging open in shock at her sister's words.

Leah didn't pay any attention to Mary Ruth's fierce look or harsh tone. Instead, she went about the business of finding her sister in order to console her. Quietly, she stole down the stairs and looked around the barn. Most of the men were still upstairs, enjoying their time together in fellowship. Several children were playing in an empty stall, jumping into a pile of fresh hay. But there was no sign of Rachel.

Walking outside, Leah found Rachel standing behind the barn, leaning against the wall and crying. A pile of old fencing hid her from view but Leah had heard her soft weeping when searching for her older sister.

"Rachel, you need to pull yourself together," Leah said

gently. "This will do no one any good."

Irritated, Rachel waved her hand at Leah. "Elijah's dying will do no one any good!" She wiped away the tears that fell from her eyes and stared at Leah. "He won't get treatment, Leah. He's just accepted this as the destination chosen for him by God!"

"He has to change his mind! He has you and the *kinner* to think about!"

"Oh, he has that all figured out," Rachel snapped, her voice sarcastic and harsh. "He told me that I should marry Menno Yoder! That God had planned Martha's death to coincide with his so that our families could join together!"

"I don't believe you!" Leah gasped. She could hardly imagine her own husband saying such a thing to her. To accept death was one thing but to tell her to marry another man, and one of *his* choosing? "He's not right in the head, Rachel. He doesn't mean it." Still, Leah mulled Rachel's words. It wasn't unusual for two families to join together in order to share the workload of raising *kinner* and crops. "He said Menno Yoder?"

Rachel shook her head. "I told him that he's being ridiculous to even think such things."

There was a brief pause in their conversation and Leah looked off to the distance. Everything was slowly turning brown as autumn was in full swing. Soon, the leaves would fall from the trees and the farmers would spread manure in the fields to prepare them for the next spring planting. Who would do Rachel's if Elijah died?

"Mayhaps you might consider such a match," Leah suggested slowly. "After a time, of course"

"Leah!" Rachel spun around and stared at her sister. Her eyes were narrow and fierce, filled with anger and disbelief. "My husband is not dead! My husband might still change his mind! And even if he doesn't, I'm not thinking of such things. Get that thought out of your mind." She lowered her head into her hands. "I'm sorry that I told you, Leah, if that's what you be thinking!"

Once again, Rachel stormed away, this time leaving Leah standing alone and staring after her, wishing that, for once, she had kept her thoughts to herself instead of letting her mouth ramble the first thing that came to her mind.

Mary Ruth had just finished drying the dishes and stacked them neatly in piles based on their design so that the women who brought them could better find their own sets in order to take them home. As she was hanging the dishtowel to dry on the edge of the sink, she felt a tugging at her skirt and turned around to see Suzanna standing there. My *dochder*, she said to herself and the words felt much more natural than she could imagine.

"Ja, sweet Suzanna? *Wie gehts?*"

"Daed told me to come find you," she said, a silly smile on her face as if she had just been told a grand secret. Leaning forward, Suzanna whispered, "Said you were going home in the buggy with us!"

Suppressing her own smile, Mary Ruth felt the color rise to her cheeks. Did the *kinner* suspect something? "*Ach vell*," she said with great flourish. "Won't that be a lovely treat? Otherwise, I'd have to walk, wouldn't I?"

Suzanna giggled and teased Mary Ruth. "It's a nice day for walking."

The sparkling glow in Suzanna's eyes warmed Mary Ruth's heart. It had been slow in coming, she thought, but the children were finally appearing to be happy again. Leaning down, Mary Ruth gently touched the little girl's arm and whispered, "But it's an even better day for a buggy ride, especially if I am with you!"

After gathering her few things, Mary Ruth quietly escaped

the kitchen and followed Suzanna down the stairs and outside to where Menno was standing next to the buggy. She hesitated, just for a brief moment, when she saw him waiting for her. His expression was soft and kind, not impatient or annoyed that he had to wait for her. She felt that same thrilling sensation when their eyes met.

He dipped his head and reached for her hand, helping her climb up into the buggy. Suzanna jumped in and sat at Mary Ruth's feet, leaning her small head against Mary Ruth's knee. Smiling at the gesture, a gesture that bespoke much of the child's comfort with her, Mary Ruth laid her hand on the girl's shoulder.

"Ready?" Menno said as he sat down on the seat next to Mary Ruth. He cast a quick glance in her direction but didn't make eye contact. With a click-click of his tongue and a slap of the reins on the horse's back, Menno drove the buggy onto the road and headed toward home.

For the first mile, no one spoke. Mary Ruth could hear the two smaller girls giggling in the back of the buggy and Melvin attempting his best to keep them quiet. Mary Ruth smiled, trying to listen to what they were saying but all she could discern was something about their daed.

"Sure is a nice autumn day," Mary Ruth finally said, breaking the silence.

Menno nodded. "Sure is."

Mary Ruth glanced out the open door of the buggy. There was a cool breeze blowing in as the horse trotted down the road. "Might be a nice day for a picnic, don't say?" she heard herself ask. No one responded. She turned to look at Menno. "Don't you think?"

She thought she saw his eyes flicker at her but he continued to stare ahead. "I reckon so," he said solemnly.

A frown crossed her face as she realized that Menno was

not taking the bait. So, instead of playing any more word games, she turned to look at Melvin and his two sisters in the back of the buggy. "What do you say, Melvin? Girls? Mayhaps I could make a batch of nice chocolate chip cookies and lemonade for a fun little rest by the stream?"

A cheer erupted from the back of the buggy and Suzanna clapped her hands. Melvin grinned at her, his smile big and telling that he knew something wonderful was happening and he liked what he suspected it was. Mary Ruth tried to hide her own smile and turned back around, looking out the window. It was going to be a wonderful day, she thought. And when she felt Menno's leg lightly brush against hers, her heart fluttered but she did not recoil, as she knew that she was where she belonged...where God wanted her to be.

The Fisher family was gathered under the large oak tree near the house. There were two large tables set up with place settings for over twenty-six people. Lizzie, Sylvia, and James had brought their families over to spend an autumn afternoon visiting with Miriam and Elias before the weather would turn cold and make long distance travel a bit more difficult.

The only ones missing were Rachel, Leah, and Mary Ruth. Anna and Lovina were in the kitchen, preparing an early evening supper for the family while Miriam and Sylvia were carrying the bowls of chow-chow, pickled cabbage and pitchers of ice water outside to the tables.

The men were outside, sitting on folding chairs near the front porch under the shade of the house while the *kinner* ran back and forth, throwing a ball for the dog to catch. John David and Steve were playing with the *kinner*, chasing some of the younger ones while Abraham, Isaac, Elias and James were discussing the latest news that they had heard from church service that morning.

"Heard that weddings will be announced next week," James said. He glanced over his shoulder at his two younger brothers. "I heard a whisper that John David and Ella will be announced."

Elias laughed. "Not a whisper you hearing, son. A right known fact, I reckon."

"Ja?"

Isaac leaned forward and winked at his brother as he teasingly said, "You need to listen closer, James. That whisper grew mighty loud a few months ago. She was even included in the circle letter that Mamm sent out. Didn't Lovina tell you?"

James raised an eyebrow. "Nee, she didn't." He frowned, a dark shadow crossing over his face. His silence spoke of something deeper than Lovina not sharing such news with him. Isaac noticed it at once.

"What troubles you, *Bruder*?"

James shrugged and looked away. His blue eyes sought the horizon, watching the sun as it began its slow descent over the backfields. Soon the fields would be plowed and manure spread over them, an annual preparation for the following year's spring planting. "Heard Eleanor Haile's been around, ain't so?" he finally said.

Both Isaac and Elias looked at each other, a silent communication passing between them.

"That she has, ja," Isaac admitted. "Little Katie is taking care of one of Eleanor's ponies at the Miller farm by Rachel and Leah's. We reckon that we'll bring the pony here for the winter, seeing that it will be too dark in the winter after school to take her there to tend to it."

A simple nod of James's head said it all. His eyes seemed to mist over as he reflected on something. Neither Isaac nor Elias had to guess very hard as to what it was he thought. It may have been years ago but the entire family remembered that James had been sweet on Eleanor Haile, prior to his taking the kneeling vow.

"Lovina seems a bit disturbed by that," James finally admitted.

"These women…" Abraham scoffed. "What crazy notions they get!"

Isaac frowned. "That was a long time ago," he said. "During your *rumschpringe*."

"I know that." James turned his face away from the setting sun and looked at his brother. "Seems to think I won't honor my marriage vow, especially since we haven't been able to…" He let his words drift, his sentence unfinished and hanging in the air.

Elias sighed. He certainly didn't like seeing his son in turmoil. Still, he didn't quite know what to say. The problem with James and Lovina had been apparent for a while, a stress from the lack of children in their marriage. "Seems some women need to have children to feel fulfilled, James. You should speak to her about adopting or doing that foster care that Jonas and Irma Miller from Paradise have done."

He waved his hand at his father. "That don't bother me none," James said. "It's the fact that she thinks such a thought. It doesn't speak well of her trust in my character." He paused and took a deep breath. "But I've said more than I should, I reckon. It's a private matter."

For a moment, none of the men spoke. No one knew what to say. Issues within the marriage remained strictly between the husband and wife. It was their way of life. If James had mentioned problems, it was surely because they were heavy and troublesome on his shoulders.

Steve walked over and joined the other men. He was out of breath but smiling. "Those *kinner* are more work than the cows," he laughed. "Easier to work in the fields!"

James looked away again.

"Think I might take a buggy ride after supper," he said casually.

Thankful for the change of subject, Isaac raised an eyebrow at his brother. "Buggy ride, ja?"

Abraham caught the teasing tone in Isaac's voice. "You don't say," he said, tugging at his graying beard. "Heard you got yourself a new buggy. Word has it that you aren't always alone in that there buggy, either!"

"You know what they say about that Amish grapevine," Steve tossed back. "Sometimes it grows sour grapes." But he laughed anyway.

The kitchen door opened and the women came out with the rest of the prepared food. Without being called, the men got up and walked to the table. The kinner noticed and hurried over, taking their place at the smaller of the two tables. When everyone was seated, they bowed their heads and said a silent blessing over their food.

Within minutes, plates were being passed, water glasses were being filled, and conversation started to flow. Miriam smiled as she looked at her family gathered around the tables. It wasn't often that so many of them came together for fellowship. Even on the holidays, trying to find a day for a Christmas dinner was hard to schedule. Inevitably, someone was always missing.

"Sure wish the other girls could have been here," Anna said.

"I was just thinking the same thing," Miriam laughed.

Lizzie looked up. "Any word on when Mary Ruth will be returning? That Menno Yoder shouldn't be needing her much longer."

Miriam sighed. "Ja, it's about that time. She needs to get back here before the weather turns. Leah sure doesn't need her help anymore, I'm sure." Her mind drifted. If anyone needed help, it was Rachel. She often wondered if Mary Ruth shouldn't just spend the winter there, helping Rachel during Elijah's illness. Yet, Miriam also knew that it wasn't fair to Mary Ruth who needed to get on with her own life. "Mayhaps I'll write a letter to Mary Ruth and have Steve drop it off. It's time."

Steve looked up at the mention of his name. "You need me to drop something off for Mary Ruth? I can head over there after supper," he volunteered a bit too eagerly. Isaac and Abraham chuckled while Anna smiled to herself.

"That Mimi Hostetler lives over that way too, ain't so?" Isaac teased.

Steve ignored him.

Anna laughed at the puzzled look on Lizzie and Lovina's faces. It was apparent that they had not heard about Steve courting anyone.

"Mayhaps I could ride along?"

The small voice that interrupted the conversation surprised everyone. It was Katie, sitting at the other table. She had overheard that Steve was going to ride over to Leah's to drop off a letter. Now, she stared at her mamm with wide eyes, eyes full of hope that her mamm would permit her this treat.

With a quick glance at Isaac who merely shrugged his shoulders, Anna nodded. "If Steve doesn't mind the company, that would be right nice, Katie. You could stop in to see Butterscotch but no grooming or riding today."

Katie's face lit up. "Oh *danke*, Mamm!"

For Katie and Steve, supper couldn't end fast enough.

"What do you mean she's not here?" Steve said, a frown on

his face. "Where is she?"

Leah was holding the baby, Jacob, while her older daughters, Edna and Emma, put away the washed dishes from supper. "I mean she's not here! She didn't come home after church service," Leah responded sharply. "Mayhaps she's over at Rachel's."

Clutching the letter in his hand, he hurried back to his buggy in order to drive across the road to Rachel's farm. The longer this took, the less time to spend with Mimi, he told himself. Plus, he had to take Katie over to the Miller's farm and pick her up again later. He hadn't counted on Katie wanting to go with him. Still, the look of joy on her face softened his heart. Clearly, Katie wanted to see her pony as much as Steve wanted to see Mimi.

Rachel was walking down the stairs when Steve entered the house. He glanced around, noticing that the *kinner* were not in the house. Elijah was seated in his chair, a blanket pulled up to his chin. His face was pale and gaunt. For a moment, Steve couldn't help but stare. He hadn't seen Elijah since that church service at Leah's. In that short period of time, his health had truly deteriorated.

"This is a surprise," Rachel said, walking between Steve and Elijah.

He shook his head, his focus on Elijah broken, and turned to look at Rachel. "I'm looking for Mary Ruth. Mamm sent a letter."

"Wrong farm," she said lightly. "She's staying at Leah's. You know that."

"Ja, right, but the thing is that she's not there," he retorted, irritated that Mary Ruth wasn't there. Each minute looking for his youngest sister was keeping him separated from Mimi. "Didn't come home after service, Leah said."

Rachel paused, setting her hands on her hips. Where could

Mary Ruth have disappeared? "That is rather odd," she said. "I saw her at church but I didn't stay for fellowship. I wanted to get back here for Elijah." She glanced at her husband. He was sleeping, oblivious to the conversation.

He handed the letter to Rachel. "Any chance you might...?" His words trailed off, a pleading look in his eyes.

"You sure are in a hurry, ain't so?" she asked suspiciously. Then, with a sigh, she reached out and took the letter. She waved it at him. "I'll get it to her."

With a big grin, Steve thanked her and hurried back outside to the buggy.

After dropping off Katie at the Miller's farm, he drove over to the Hostetler home. His mind was in a whirl. He barely paid any attention to where he was going. Luckily, the horse seemed to know his way to Mimi's house. Steve was too distracted, the scene replaying his mind of what he had just witnessed on the way to the Miller's farm.

They had turned left at the end of Rachel's lane and were headed down the road. When they turned the corner by the Yoder's farm, Katie had waved franticly from the buggy at a group of six people walking down the road with a picnic basket. Steve blinked and tried to focus on the people. When he finally realized that he recognized the woman as his sister, he pulled back on the reins and stopped the buggy. "Whoa," he said to the horse, his voice soothing but his mind still not comprehending that his sister was walking with the Yoder's down the street.

"Mary Ruth!" he called out.

She turned around, startled that her brother had called her from the buggy that just passed them. "Steve?" She glanced at the man next to her, the man that Steve recognized as Menno Yoder. He nodded at Mary Ruth before she left his side and hurried to the buggy. "Whatever are you doing here?"

He frowned and glanced over her shoulder at the happy little family standing there, waiting for Mary Ruth to rejoin them. "I might be asking you the same thing," he murmured so that no one but Mary Ruth could hear. "No one could find you."

"*Vell,*" she said, her tone short and clipped. "I am an adult."

Steve ignored her remark. "Mamm sent a letter. I left it with Rachel."

Mary Ruth raised an eyebrow. "Everything all right at home then?"

"Ja," he said slowly. "But Mamm says it's time for you to come home." Steve glanced over her shoulder at Menno, surprised that he was watching them so intently. Even the children were crowded around Menno, waiting. "He seems to be doing better."

It was the look on Mary Ruth's face that told Steve what he had suspected when he first recognized her walking alongside Menno Yoder. She didn't say anything but the color drained from her face. Her silence spoke volumes. And he knew: *Mary Ruth wasn't going to be returning home.*

"Steve?"

He snapped out of his thoughts and saw Mimi staring at him. For a moment, he was dazed and had to look around himself. He barely remembered driving down her lane and he certainly didn't remember stopping his horse and buggy by the hitching rail in front of the barn.

"You sick?" she asked, concern written across her face.

"*Nee, nee,*" he said and jumped out of the buggy. "I just saw something…" he started to say but his voice trailed off as he walked alongside Mimi toward the house. "I can't even describe it."

"Ja vell, you sure look like you saw something," she said, frowning. "You look like you saw a specter!"

He shook his head. "Nothing like that. But it was just as odd. I saw my sister walking with Menno Yoder down the lane," he said.

At this, Mimi looked equally as surprised. "Menno Yoder?"

"You don't think that..." He couldn't complete the sentence. How could he suspect that his sister, so young and vibrant, would be courting not just an older man but a widower with four children at that!

"So soon? I mean Menno was crazy about Martha. I don't think he'd be showing interest in someone so quickly," Mimi whispered. The thought horrified her. Could Menno truly replace his love for Martha that fast? "But then again..." This time, Mimi couldn't finish her sentence.

"What?"

"*Vell*," she began. "He has been looking less forlorn at church service these past few weeks. And the *kinner* adore your sister. It will be tough for Menno to raise them alone, especially the girls. They need a mamm."

A silence fell between them, leaving them to their inner thoughts. Men needed wives. Women needed husbands. It was a plain fact. Yet, it was discomforting to think that it could happen so quickly. Steve wanted to tell Mimi that he would never do such a thing. Without Mimi, he'd be lost. But the words wouldn't form on his lips. He couldn't make a promise that he didn't know if he could keep. What if something dreadful happened to Mimi? What if he one day found he was left alone with four young ones and a farm to tend?

"It's awful quick, ain't so?" Steve asked.

At that statement, Mimi laughed and playfully touched his arm. "No more so than us, ja?"

There was truth in her statement and he couldn't help himself from smiling. It had been just right before Martha Yoder's accident when he had first met Mimi Hostetler and they had started courting shortly thereafter.

They were inside the kitchen, enjoying a cold drink and fresh apple crisp when the door opened and Mimi's daed walked inside.

"Might want to come see this, Steve," he said, his eyes twinkling.

Outside, Steve immediately noticed that something was missing. Mimi followed close behind, grabbing her shawl from the peg on the wall as the evening air was beginning to get cool. She, too, noticed that something was wrong.

"Where's my buggy?" Steve exclaimed, realizing that the horse was gone.

Jonas laughed. "Oh, don't you fret none. It's coming back."

Steve frowned, wondering if Mimi's daed was getting ferhoodled. "Coming back? From where? I left it right there!" he said, pointing toward the hitching rail.

As he said it, he could hear the noise of horse hooves on the road and the rattling of the buggy wheels. Mimi looked down the road, squinting as she tried to make out who was coming up the driveway but the setting sun was too bright to make out the driver.

"What in the world...?" Steve hurried toward the driveway and saw a young man walking his horse up the lane. In the buggy, sitting perfectly straight on the front seat, was Shep, Isaac and Anna's dog.

Laughing, Jonas followed Steve. "Was out front over yonder and saw the buggy go by. That horse sure did seem to know where she was going! And lo and behold, there was that dog sitting in the front seat, natural as could be!"

"How'd you get the horse?" Steve asked the young man who was holding the horse by the bridle.

He shrugged. "Saw it approaching and realized dogs can't

drive horses. Managed to get her to stop before she passed."

Mimi caught up with the men and laughed at the sight. The dog was still sitting on the front seat, panting happily at the attention he was receiving.

"I've seen everything now," Mimi said as she approached the side of the buggy. "Where did you come from?" She petted the dog and looked over at Steve questioningly.

He pulled off his straw hat and scratched his head. Clearly, he was as wonderstruck as the rest. "I wouldn't believe it if I didn't see it myself!" He ran his hand down the mare's neck, kicking himself for surely he had forgotten to tie her to the hitching rail. He had been too distracted by his encounter with Mary Ruth. The horse must have wandered off and, when realizing she wasn't tied down, tried her old trick of heading back home.

"And with the dog?"

Steve laughed. "I had heard that he's been sleeping in the buggies of late. Isaac's Anna found him a few times, curled up in the back, sound asleep, when she goes shopping at market. He must've been there the entire time I was looking for Mary Ruth!"

Jonas tied the horse to the hitching rail while Steve thanked the neighbor.

Once back inside the house, Jonas sat down at the kitchen table and gestured for Steve to join him. "Well, son, beside having a crazy horse and a lazy dog, I understand there is other more important news you might want to be sharing with me prior to the next church service," he said, his eyes sparkling at the man who was to become his son-in-law.

Steve was caught off guard by how frank and direct Jonas was. He had never thought that he would need to speak to Jonas about marrying Mimi. It was something that was announced in church and discussed immediately afterward.

"Ja vell," he began, searching for the words to begin. "I

reckon that Mimi told you then?" He glanced at her and she tried to hide her smile. A faint hint of pink covered her cheeks and Steve could see that, clearly, she was as excited and happy as he was. He turned back to Jonas and took a deep breath. "I'd like to marry your *dochder*, ja."

"Hear you have yourself a farm over by your daed's farm."

Steve nodded. "Just across the road."

Jonas seemed to mull this over. Clearly something was on Jonas' mind, something that made him less than happy about the marriage. Steve began to feel panicky, wondering if Mimi's daed would have some objection to their marriage. Certainly his own reputation was right gut. And he was a good Amish man. Whatever could be troubling her daed?

"You have a concern?" Steve asked, not wanting to beat around the bush.

Leaning back in the chair, Jonas rubbed his chin. "She's not used to farm life, you know," he began. "Used to working in the store with me. Farm life..." He paused, his eyes searching the air and avoiding Steve's. "Farm life is hard, Steve. Hard on the farmer and hard on his *fraa*."

That wasn't what he expected. Steve wondered where her daed was going with this. Certainly he didn't object to their marriage! After all, it wasn't up to the parents to grant permission. "It can be, yes," he admitted slowly.

"Daed," Mimi said softly, rolling her eyes. "We already had this talk."

Her daed lifted his hand to gently silence her. "I'm entitled to have my say, Mimi," he scolded but in a loving tone. "Marriage is forever and I want my *dochder* taken care of," he said.

Steve lifted his head, stunned at John's words. Did Mimi's daed actually think that he wouldn't take care of her? "If you have an objection..." Steve started, trying to keep his heart calm and temper calmer. "I'd like to know what it is."

Jonas shook his head slowly. "*Nee*," he said. "I have no objections, Steve. Not to you. Besides, I reckon it's not my place to say so, if I did. I just want you to be easy on her. It will take her some time to adapt to farm life."

For a moment, Steve didn't quite know what to say. Farm life was all that he had ever known. He didn't know any other life and, from that perspective, didn't understand what Jonas meant. He wished that he had something to say, a way to respond to Jonas. But he didn't.

"Daed," Mimi said with confidence. "I'll be just fine."

But Jonas' words echoed in Steve's head: *I want you to be easy on her*. Was life on a farm so very different that her daed was worried? True, there were no vacations on a farm. No days off. Still, the routine was more on his shoulders than on hers. From what he knew about Mimi, she was good-natured and hard working. Together, they'd be able to succeed. Of that, he was sure and certain. Many years ago, he had given up hope of finding such a partner. Until the day that he had laid eyes on Mimi and he had not felt her objecting to it.

Steve took a deep breath and leveled his gaze at Jonas. "Jonas, I promise that I will care for your *dochder* with the most tender love and understanding possible. I'll help her adjust to life on a farm and to the daily routine. And I'll do what I can to see that she has a *wunderbaar gut* life, a godly life. After all, God is our refuge and strength." He turned to look at Mimi and felt a wave of warmth flow through him. Relief. Love. Awe. He wasn't certain what he was feeling, perhaps a mixture of it all. But he sensed that she was embracing his words as well. As she met his gaze, he smiled. "Together and with God, we will both be right gut."

She took a step forward and laid her hand on his shoulder.

Jonas clapped his hands once and stood up from the table. "That's what I like to hear, son!" He clapped Steve on the back in a friendly gesture of familiarity. "We welcome you to the family, then. Should be a lonely house without Mimi here but I reckon you are close enough that she will stop by frequently." He paused. "Both of you."

He walked toward the door, reaching for his hat.

"You speak with the bishop yet?" he asked as he stood at the kitchen door. "Announcements are at next service. You will need to let him know and decide on a date. I'll have Mimi and her mamm put together the list for inviting folks."

Steve nodded. *This is real,* he thought. *I'm actually getting married.* "I will leave the date up to Mimi," he said.

Unfortunately, he knew that it didn't really matter since his tenants were still in the farmhouse. He had spoken with them just the day before and they were going to look to move in the spring or as soon as they could find a new place to rent. Mimi would continue to live with her parents after the wedding and they would go visiting relatives on the weekends. Worse case scenario, he knew that he could fix up the small apartment in the back of the main house until his tenants could find a place. But that would have to wait for warmer weather.

"Can I tell you a secret?" Melvin asked as he hung on the side of the stall door, watching Katie grooming Butterscotch. He knew that she shouldn't be grooming the pony on a Sunday but it didn't bother him none. He was just glad that his daed had granted him permission to run over to the Miller's farm to visit with her.

"A secret?" she asked, her eyes wide and bright.

"Ja!" He reached into his pocket. "I found something that you might want to see." He took a crumpled piece of paper out of his pocket and opened it. "Here," he said ,thrusting it at her.

Katie left the side of the pony and reached for the paper. It was a letter. The handwriting was neat and elegant. It was also familiar. "That's Mary Ruth's handwriting!" she exclaimed and looked up. "Where did you find this?"

He looked sheepish as if he suddenly regretted showing it to her. He hadn't thought she'd react like that. "It was by the trash bin. But read what the note says."

Katie frowned and tried to hand it back to him. "That's private!"

Melvin pushed her hand away. "Read it!"

Reluctantly, she let her eyes skim over the letter. When she got to the second paragraph, her eyes grew wide and she looked up at Melvin. "Oh," she whispered.

He smiled. "Ja!" He reached for the note. "Mary Ruth's going to be my new mamm."

"That would make us cousins!" Katie said, not certain if she was excited or not. Hadn't her grossmammi just sent a letter telling Mary Ruth it was time to come home? Who else knew about this? "You feel gut about having a new mamm?"

Melvin shrugged his shoulders and glanced at the ground. "I know she won't be my Mamm. No one can replace her. But it would sure be nice to see my daed happy again and Mary Ruth is right *gut* to all of us."

"Do you sisters know?"

He nodded. "Suzanna does. I didn't tell the little ones," he admitted. "They'd talk."

Katie pursed her lips, thinking for a moment. It hadn't been that long since Mary Ruth was taking care of Melvin, Suzanna, Ruth Ann, and Emma. How long had Menno been courting her? Hadn't his wife just died four or so months ago? "Are they in love?" Katie asked, staring at Melvin as if he had the answer.

He blushed and looked away. "I don't know nothing about that!"

"I wonder what it feels like to be in love," she said absentmindedly, gazing out the barn door. "I imagine it must be how I feel when I'm around Butterscotch."

At that, Melvin looked at her. Butterscotch? The pony?

If only he could tell her that he knew exactly how it felt to be in love. It was a wonderful feeling, a feeling of warmth and joy from the moment he was standing close to her until the moment they had to part. Love overcame everything…every thought, every breath. He was happy when he was with her and, when they were apart, he could find happiness thinking about her. He lived in the memories of her teaching him to ride Butterscotch or showing him how she had taught the pony to jump over small logs. When she laughed, her face lit up and his heart would sing.

How could she compare love to what she felt for an animal?

"I reckon," he mumbled. "I best get going. My daed will wonder where I am." He didn't wait for her reply before he hurried out the door.

She watched him leave and wondered what she had said. With a heavy heart, she put the grooming brush away and wandered outside to sit on a hay bale and wait for Steve to pick her up. Without Melvin to keep her company, it just wasn't the same. After all, it was Melvin who made being around Butterscotch so special.

Chapter 10: Miriam's Package

She sat on the church bench, her heart pounding inside of her chest and a lump forming in her throat. Several people were looking at her discreetly and whispering to each other. She didn't blame them. It was all that she could do to keep staring straight ahead and not seek out Elias from where he sat across the room. She knew that if she had looked at him, Miriam would burst out in tears.

They had known about John David and Ella. That was a given. They had suspected about Steve and Mimi Hostetler, although Steve had been very private about his courtship and only informed them earlier that week that the deacon would be announcing their upcoming wedding.

But Mary Ruth?

When she had heard the deacon announce that her daughter was getting married, it took her a minute to comprehend his words. Mary Ruth? And then she heard the name Menno Yoder and she felt as if the bottom of her world had collapsed. *How could this have happened?*

The date had been set already. Ten days. One week from Tuesday. It was unheard of. At least, this was what Miriam thought. As far as her memory served her well, it was unheard of for a couple to announce the wedding and the date without talking to their parents first. However, since Menno was a widower, maybe the rules were different. She just didn't know.

What she did know was that she had a headache and pain in her jaw from clenching her teeth so tightly.

Miriam tried to act natural, not wanting anyone to know that she had just been completely shocked at the news. In fact, from the expressions on other people's faces, they were as shocked as she was. Still, she didn't want them to think that she hadn't known a thing. Nor did she want them to think that she didn't approve. After all, the deacon had announced it and it was now official

"Well," Lizzie Petersheim said after the service, "Three weddings in one season!" She was holding her three-month-old baby, smiling at Miriam. "Sure took me by surprise, though. It's only been what? Four? Five months?"

Miriam caught her breath and, rather than answer, changed the conversation by cooing over the baby. "You sure must be pleased with this darling one," she said. "How many is that now? Four?"

Lizzie smiled, pleased with the praise for her baby. "Five."

"And one day, you too shall have weddings in your home for them, ja?" Miriam hoped that she sounded genuinely excited, that she was masking the piercing pain in her heart from her youngest daughter's decision without any discussion with or consideration of, her parents. *Ten days,* she thought. Did Mary Ruth expect to marry in Miriam's home? Or was she doing something else unconventional?

"Congratulations, Miriam," someone else said at her elbow. "You let me know what I can do to help."

"*Danke*, Ruth," Miriam replied, glancing around the room for Elias. Her head was throbbing and she had to get out of the room. Despite the post-service fellowship hour, she knew that she couldn't stay there for one more minute. "Have you seen Elias yet? I'm feeling a bit poorly. Want to leave," she said.

Fifteen minutes later, she was seated in the buggy next to her husband. Alone and away from prying eyes, she let the tears fall down her cheeks. Elias stared straight ahead, the reins taunt in his hands. He let his wife pour out her emotions without consoling her. He knew better. She needed time to collect her thoughts and decide a course of action.

"We need to go to her," Miriam finally said. "Now. Right now, Elias."

Without saying a word, he nodded his head and steered the horse and buggy past the turn for their farm and headed across town toward Rachel and Leah's.

Mary Ruth had left the building just after the deacon had announced the upcoming weddings. She avoided her sisters' glares but could certainly feel the tension in the room. She had known that the reactions from people would be mixed. After all, Martha Yoder had been part of their community for many years. Now, Menno was taking a new bride. It was understandable that people would raise an eyebrow, especially since Mary Ruth had been helping with the *kinner* since Martha's accident. Who knew what thoughts were crossing their minds!

"Mary Ruth!"

Mary Ruth stopped walking and turned around, surprised to see Menno jogging to catch up with her.

"You aren't staying for the fellowship meal then?" he asked as he approached her. When he stood before her, he reached out and touched her arm. "People will want to wish you well, ja?"

"*Nee*," she said, shaking her head. The other couples that had been announced hadn't attended at all that day. At that moment, she wished that she hadn't attended, either, but being that she was marrying a widower, the rules were different. "I feel most uncomfortable in there. I can hear their tongues wagging already."

He laughed, his hand still resting on her arm. "No tongues are wagging."

Mary Ruth made a face. "Rachel and Leah seemed none too pleased."

"Come back," he said gently. There was an understanding look in his eye, a sense of compassion that immediately put her at ease. "It will look odd if you disappear. Mayhaps that you are none too pleased yourself."

At this, she smiled and felt the color creeping onto her cheeks. Menno sure had a way of making her blush.

The past two weeks had flown by. Each morning, it was all that she could do to not race through her chores at Leah's in order to hurry to the Yoder farm. Since their conversation at the last church service, Mary Ruth had seen a remarkable difference in Menno. He spent more time in the house when she was there, even taking breaks with the barn chores to visit with her in the kitchen.

Once, he had even reached across the table and, after the slightest of hesitations, he had touched her hand. She had never had a man make such a gesture and the feel of his thumb gently caressing her skin sent a thrill through her veins. She had to pull her hand back and avert her eyes, but not before she saw the look of amusement on his face. That, too, had caused her to blush.

She could scarcely believe that this man, this wonderful man, was the same shell of a person she had met not so long ago. Gone were the fierce stares and harsh words. Instead, he was soft spoken and gentle, kind and attentive. With the commitment made for their union, he had slipped into a mode of pleased acceptance and pure contentment that she would never have thought possible. And with this, she knew that he loved her.

Of course, she also knew that his love for her was at the infancy stage. It wasn't as deep as what he had felt for Martha. But she was hopeful that, given some more time, it would grow. If only, she thought, she could feel confident that he would never compare her to Martha, his first true love. She prayed that he would have enough room in his heart to love her just as much, even if in a different way.

"I'm pleased," she finally said, aware that he was watching her intensely and with pleading eyes. "But I'm not ready for the questions from my sisters."

He reached for her hand and held it tightly. "Then let me

take you to them. We can face them together."

She looked up in surprise. *Together?* Where had this man been for the past few months? His gentleness and soft tone stunned her. She had never heard another Amish man speak this way to his wife, although she knew that she had never heard private conversations between married couples. *Is this what it will be like?* For a moment, her knees felt weak. "Oh Menno," she whispered, feeling her reluctance dissolve

He squeezed her hand briefly then, letting it go, he placed his hand on her shoulder and gently guided her back to the large room over the barn where the fellowship meal was about to take place.

"Do you believe this?" Leah hissed under her breath to Rachel. "I'm speechless! She didn't even tell us."

"I sure hope she knows what she is doing," Rachel sighed. "She's awful young to be a mamm to those *kinner*."

"It's so soon! Martha only died in the early summer!"

Rachel clicked her tongue, disapprovingly. Still, her mind wandered to her own husband and his demand that she'd consider marrying Menno when he passed. It wasn't uncommon for a husband to suggest such a thing and Rachel knew that it would have been a potential solution to the farm situation. With Elijah refusing treatment, the inevitable was bound to happen. She would become a young widow with a large farm to tend to and no farmer to do so. Perhaps her unhappiness with Mary Ruth marrying Menno was because she was worried about her own future and had considered Elijah's suggestion?

She shook her head. *He's not dead*, she scolded herself. *There is still a chance.* "*Vell*, if this is what she wants and what God has planned for her, then we must support her," Rachel forced the words from her lips. "And, she will be living in our district which is right nice, ja?"

Leah waved her hand at Rachel. "Mother of four, at that age? She'll be needing us close by for advice, that's for sure and certain!"

Rachel changed the subject. "What about the other one? That Steve!" This time, she smiled. Besides the shock of Mary Ruth and Menno's upcoming marriage, the congregation was also buzzing about Mimi Hostetler getting married to their brother. "I had wondered why he bought that buggy but I never suspected Mimi to be the reason!"

Leah scoffed. "Seems our siblings are right *gut* about keeping secrets, ain't so!"

The voices in the large room seemed to shift and Rachel looked up in time to see Mary Ruth and Menno walk through the doorway. She hadn't even noticed that her sister had left. Clenching her jaw, she lifted her chin and approached the couple to offer her congratulations. Still, she couldn't help but feel a tinge of envy that her youngest sister had somehow won the heart of Menno Yoder, a man much older than her and already established with his own farm and family. It just didn't seem fair when her own world was falling apart so quickly.

Instead of attending church service, Steve had picked up Mimi from her home. It was official. They were to be married in three weeks from Thursday. He knew that many members of the congregation were certainly surprised, both at his church and at hers, when the deacons had announced it. He was grateful that they did not have to attend the service on that day. Instead, the young couples were allowed to enjoy dinner alone at their mamm's houses, a time to be alone and talk while the rest of the community learned about their engagement.

Mimi had packed a picnic lunch at Steve's request. Now, as they drove along the tortuous road, they seemed giddy with excitement, knowing that their engagement was finally public knowledge.

"Three weeks," Steve said, holding Mimi's hand while they drove down the road.

She laughed and leaned against him. "I'm so happy," she whispered.

"Did your mamm make the list? I'll have to start visiting people to invite them this next week," he said. It was pat of the ritual. The groom would travel the district, dropping off invitations to the family, friends, and church members. Between the two households, there would be close to 400 people in attendance at their wedding, which would be held at Mimi's parents' house.

Mimi laughed again. "Did she make the list? She had the list done the same night that she found out!"

He laughed with her, pleased that her mamm was overjoyed. After all, starting the guest list right away was paramount to an immediate approval!

She hadn't asked where he was taking her but suspected she knew the answer when he crossed over the main road and drove the horse down a side lane. It was a beautiful day with the sun shining through the trees, covered with multi-colored leaves. In just another week or so, the leaves would certainly start falling, layering the ground in a blanket of reds, oranges, and yellows.

By the time they were to wed, the trees would be bare and winter at their doorstep.

"I thought you'd like to see your future home," he said as he pulled the buggy into a driveway.

She smiled and looked around. "Is this it?" she asked, taking in the pretty white farmhouse and long white dairy barn. The smell of the cows hit her nose and she winced for just a moment. It was strong and pungent, a touch of acidity to it. "Suppose that it will take time to get used to," she teased.

He raised an eyebrow. "What?"

"The smell from the cows."

He chuckled and shrugged his shoulders. "I don't even notice it anymore. At least I don't have pigs!" They both laughed, knowing that the smell from a cow barn was nothing compared to that of a hog farm.

He stopped the buggy and helped her climb down before he made certain to properly hitch the horse to the rail. He turned around and watched as Mimi stood there, staring at everything. The garden was behind the house, already cleared from the previous summer harvest. The house had a wraparound porch with a swing that just begged of future family evenings with a glass of meadow tea, sharing the details of the day with Steve.

She took a step toward the barn and peeked inside the door. "Look at all of these cows! Whose cows are they?"

Steve followed her, pausing to push the door open further so that they could walk inside. "Some are mine, some belong to the tenants. He'll take his herd when he finds a new farm. We'll buy some more in the spring and breed some of the ones that I already have."

She nodded.

He took her hand and led her down the aisle between the wall and the cows. "Between the fields and the cows, we'll have a lot of work to do but I'll remember my promise to your daed, Mimi."

"Promise?"

He stopped walking and turned to look at her. *Had she forgotten already,* he wondered. "My promise that I'll help you to adapt to being a farmer's wife." He lifted his hand and gently touched her cheek. "We are a team," he whispered and, with just the slightest of hesitations, he leaned down and brushed his lips against her, the first and last first kiss for both of them.

When he pulled away, she averted her eyes and lowered her head. He chuckled to himself and lifted her chin so that she had no choice but to meet his gaze.

"You blush over a kiss?" he asked softly. "With your soon-to-be husband?"

She shook her head. "*Nee*," she responded. "I blush over how you make me feel."

"Ah," he said, a twinkle in his eyes. "God arranged for us to meet last summer, Mimi. It was His plan and what you are feeling is the Lord moving inside you, telling you that you are walking the very path He intended for you. For us." He paused and smiled. "I feel that same way. It's God telling us how pleased He is that we listened to Him."

"God's plan," she repeated softly and nodded. That was exactly how she was feeling. Nervous? A little. Excited? Yes. Confident? Absolutely. "Yes, I believe you are right, Steve."

He lifted her hand to his lips and kissed it. "Now, let's go look at the house. The tenants said it would be OK if I brought you over to walk you through it so that you could start planning for furniture and housewares. They even invited us for supper, although we might decline so that we can visit with your parents and I can get that long list of people to invite."

With a jovial bounce to his step, he pulled her alongside him as they hurried to the house. For Mimi, it was the first time that she would enter the house where her future laid. For Steve, it was the next step in his life, one that he had never thought would come to fruition: the day that he took his intended through the home that he had dreamed would soon become a home full of laughter, love, and life.

Mary Ruth hadn't expected her parents to show up at Menno's farm after the church service. She had returned home with him to start preparing the list of guests to invite to the wedding. The *kinner* were laughing and getting excited, crowding around Mary Ruth and teasingly calling her Mamm. Even Menno seemed relaxed and at ease with the family scene that unfolded in the kitchen.

So when Miriam and Elias walked into the house, a silence befell the room, interrupting the moment of joy and happiness. The *kinner* crowded around Mary Ruth, little Emma crawling onto her lap and burying her face against Mary Ruth's shoulder.

"*Gut nochmidawk*," Menno said, taking a step forward to reach out and shake Elias' hand, welcoming them to his home.

Reluctantly, Elias returned the gesture.

"Mary Ruth," Miriam started. "Might we have a word in private with you and Menno?"

Mary Ruth frowned, caught off guard by the unexpected visit as well as her mother's peculiar request. She set Emma on the ground and turned to Melvin. "Mayhaps you could take the girls to the barn and check on those kittens, ja?" She didn't wait for him to nod his head and take Emma by the hand, quietly and obediently leading his sisters out of the kitchen.

The adults waited until the outside door shut behind the *kinner*. The room was silent, the only noise being the soft tick-tock of the clock that hung on the wall by the sitting area.

It was Miriam who started, taking a deep breath before she said, "I understand that you have an announcement, Mary Ruth. At what point were you going to discuss it with us?"

Trying to appear non-perplexed, Mary Ruth kept her shoulders squared and lifted her chin. "I tried to write you a letter," she said. "It just didn't come out right."

"And hearing of this from the deacon, that's right?" Miriam

asked, her voice sounding irritated although she was trying to remain calm. "Ten days?"

Menno cleared his throat. "Mayhaps I was wrong for not coming to talk to you," he said apologetically. "Under the circumstances, I didn't right think about it."

"Circumstances?" Miriam asked, her face paling. "Oh help," she said, clutching her chest and sinking into a chair.

"Nee, nee," Mary Ruth said, reaching forward to touch her mamm's hand. "It's nothing like that! Do you truly think so little of me?"

Understanding the hidden insinuation, Menno stepped up again. "Miriam, Elias, please understand that Mary Ruth has been living out here with her sisters. This happened very quickly and, being that it is my second marriage and I'm not a young man, I hadn't given thought to approaching you. I forget that Mary Ruth is…" His voice trailed off.

"Is what?" Miriam asked sharply. "Quite young to become a mamm to your *kinner*? She could practically be their older sister, Menno."

"Miriam," Elias said gently, placing his hand on his wife's shoulder. "We have to trust that Mary Ruth and Menno have discussed these issues. We have to believe that this is the Lord's will and we must support them."

"I love the *kinner*," Mary Ruth said forcefully. "They need a mamm and I want to be their mamm."

Miriam snapped, her gaze going from Menno to her daughter. "Love the *kinner*?" She exhaled sharply. "What about the father? Do you love *him*?"

"Miriam!"

She ignored Elias and stared at Mary Ruth, waiting for an answer. But the expected answer did not come out in the open. Mary Ruth looked away, wishing she was brave enough to shout

out "Yes, I do!" But those were private thoughts and not something she wished to share with her parents. She hadn't even expressed that to Menno, waiting for a moment when he, too, would be comfortable telling her how he truly felt. She only prayed that, one day, she would hear those words from his lips. So, rather than confirm how she truly felt, Mary Ruth simply replied, "We are right *gut* friends, Mamm. That's all you need to know."

Miriam shook her head. "Well, I shall pray to the good Lord that friendship is the start, then," she reluctantly replied. It was all that she could say for, in her heart, she felt that Mary Ruth was rushing into this marriage, but truth be told, she was now an adult and parents did not have to bless the union. "And where, pray tell, will you be having this wedding in ten days?"

"Here," Menno answered for Mary Ruth. "We want to have it here, at our home."

"Here?" Miriam covered her mouth with her hand. That explained why the date was announced without talking to her and Elias first. Most weddings were held in the bride's house. Why would they choose Menno's home?

Menno could see that she was confused. He pulled the chair out from under the table and sat down next to Mary Ruth. "We want new and *gut* memories to be born again out of this house. We want people to see this as Mary Ruth's home now. It's a second marriage for me and, I'd have a smaller gathering except for the fact that Mary Ruth is young and this is her first marriage. We want to celebrate and have joy in the house that so recently was filled with such sorrow. Sorrow that your daughter has helped us all to overcome and for which I am very grateful. We all feel that Mary Ruth is part of this family. "

For the first time, Elias spoke. "Menno, Mary Ruth," he began. "I wish you well in this marriage. I understand the reasons behind it and, though surprised, I can see that you have both worked together to plan it." He ignored the sharp look from

Miriam. "A marriage born of friendship is destined to be strong. So, while I am a bit taken aback by how fast this has happened, I can honestly say that I support this marriage and I am happy to welcome you and your *kinner* to the family."

Miriam started to turn to look at him, ready to contradict what he said, but he squeezed her shoulder, avoiding her look. As the head of the family, Elias' word was final. If he accepted the marriage, she would have to accept it as well. With a reluctant sigh, she knew that the fight was over, if indeed there had been anything to fight. Instead, it was time to start planning a wedding.

Elijah hadn't taken the news of Mary Ruth and Menno's wedding in good stride. Instead, he seemed to sink further into depression. When Rachel told him the news that had been announced at church service, he had all but sworn under his breath. His brow had furrowed together in a scowl and he looked away from his wife.

"Should've been you," he had mumbled.

"Stop that," she had snapped back. "If you'd only get the treatment, we might not have to worry about this!" She hated the tone in her voice and immediately regretted the anger she had felt.

For several days, he didn't speak to anyone in the house. Instead, he continued to decline as he withered away in his chair. Rachel did her best to milk the cows and tend to the barn chores along side her older sons. Slowly, however, she noticed that the house was becoming dirty, laundry was piling up, and things were simply just starting to fall apart.

When the important chores were finished, she headed over to Leah's, hoping to escape the doom and gloom that lingered over her household. While the children were at school, it was unbearable to stay there, watching her husband slowly die.

Leah's house wasn't much better. The baby cried incessantly as his teeth were starting to break through his gum line. Leah simply rocked him all day, not tending to the house chores. Her own husband avoided spending much time at home, most likely disgusted with how Leah focused all of her attention on baby Jacob and none of her attention on her responsibilities around the house. Rachel started to take over the kitchen duties, cleaning her sister's house rather than her own.

As the weekend approached, they also started cooking for the wedding that was just days away. Bread needed to be baked. Pies needed to be made. Casseroles needed to be prepared.

No one spoke negatively about Mary Ruth's upcoming marriage or the unconventional manner in which she was approaching the wedding. The rest of the church district didn't seem to care that the wedding service would be held at Menno's house. For a second marriage, some of the traditions were often modified. In fact, after getting over their initial surprise and gossip about the suddenness of the marriage, many of the older church members thought that the union made good sense, at least for Menno.

Miriam had insisted on coming over to help Mary Ruth clean the house from top to bottom. While the *kinner* were at school, Mary Ruth spent her days at Menno Yoder's house with her mamm, scrubbing the walls and floors, washing the window shades and shaking out the sheer white curtains. Every inch of the house was cleaned and re-organized so that it had, in fact, transformed into a new home.

By Friday, Miriam insisted that Mary Ruth return home. It was time to work on her wedding dress. A simple pale blue fabric was purchased from Miller's Dry Goods Store and Miriam attacked the task with full steam. By Saturday evening, the dress was finished and Mary Ruth took her time pressing it, being certain to use extra starch so that there was no worry about any wrinkles. She also bleached and starched her prayer kapp, taking extra care to iron the strings that would hang over her shoulders, tied in a loose, neat bow at her throat.

"You are supposed to spend your wedding night here," Miriam said, her voice full of reproach. "You always have to do things your own way, don't you?"

"Mamm, please stop," her daughter answered, rolling her eyes.

"I just don't see why you couldn't have waited until spring," Miriam snapped. "More and more couples are doing that, now! It would have been more proper to the memory of Martha!"

"Mamm!"

Mary Ruth spun around, tired of hearing the criticism. Her mamm had never been so vocal with displeasure over anything. It was beginning to grate on Mary Ruth's nerves, especially since she knew that it was not proper for her mamm to be so negative about the wedding.

"You know the reason why," she said. "The *kinner* need a mamm. A real mamm. Besides, I'm working there anyway. It wouldn't be proper to continue that arrangement. People would talk."

"Oh, they are talking already and that doesn't seem to bother you none!" Miriam said, her hands on her hips.

"Then let them talk," Mary Ruth said dismissively. Three more days and this would all be behind her. No more idle gossip. No more dealing with her mamm. "Their gossip speaks more about them than it does about me."

Miriam sighed. There was no use fighting Mary Ruth. After all, in three days, she would be married to Menno Yoder, whether Miriam liked it or not. Accept it, she told herself. Certainly Mary Ruth would encounter bumps in the road like any other new bride. She'd need her mamm then for advice. "I reckon you're right, Mary Ruth."

"Now," Mary Ruth said, taking charge of the situation. "Are we certain we will have enough food?"

Once again, they went over the list of who was bringing what food to the wedding meal. Unlike a regular wedding with 400 people attending, the fact that this was Menno's second marriage meant that there was less involvement from the community. Mary Ruth's family would attend as would Menno's siblings that lived nearby. Most of the church members would come, too. However, if there was another wedding on the same day, it would take precedence. Mary Ruth figured that 200 people would attend, possibly 250. By Amish standards, it was a smaller wedding. For that, she was grateful. She was nervous enough about marrying Menno Yoder, a man she had only just begun to know. It took some pressure off of her that the celebration and festivities would be tempered down a bit.

The sky was overcast on Tuesday morning. Mary Ruth hadn't been able to sleep. It was her last night staying at Leah's. Despite her mother wanting her to stay at home, Mary Ruth had refused, saying that it felt less like home anymore and besides, she argued, she didn't want to be worried about getting to the wedding service on time. Her mamm and daed's farm was almost a twenty-minute buggy ride away from Menno Yoder's place.

It was just like a regular church service. She hadn't been to the house since the previous week and she was pleased that the *kinner* and Menno had kept it spotless. The furniture was moved out and, in its place, were the familiar church benches, lined up in such a way that the men would sit on one side and the women on another, facing them.

The service opened with singing. One of the men started the hymn, singing the first syllable of the hymn in a long, drawn out singsong manner. The rest of the congregation joined in. Mary

Ruth found herself mouthing the words but no sound came out. She was nervous, her hands shaking as she realized that, in less than three hours, by the end of the service, she would be Menno Yoder's wife.

If she had ever doubted herself and the decision, this was the moment.

Her hands felt sweaty and she wondered how pale her face looked. It was hot in the room and she glanced at one of the windows. It was opened but she felt no breeze. For a brief moment, she contemplated getting up and stepping outside. She needed air as her head felt light and dizzy. *What am I doing,* she asked herself.

Time seemed to stand still. The singing was still on the first verse. There were five more verses to sing. She wanted to shift her weight on the bench but worried that people would notice her and think she was fidgeting. Only children fidgeted and certainly not young women dressed in blue for their wedding day.

She looked up and glanced around the room.

He was watching her, his hand touching his chin just above his whiskers. There was a look of concern on his face. Menno must have been able to read her mind, she thought. When their eyes met, she saw him nod just ever so slightly and gesture with his hand that she should relax.

And so it worked. She took a deep breath and exhaled, not caring whether or not the women seated along side of her had noticed it. When she looked back at Menno, he gave her a soft smile then directed his attention back to the front of the room. Mary Ruth watched him for just another moment, feeling a tug at her heart. His attentiveness and ability to read her emotions helped her remain strong. *He is a right gut man*, she told herself. *God led me to Menno. It is His will that brought us together.*

It was just after eleven when the bishop stood before the congregation. He slowly looked around the room before he asked Menno and Mary Ruth to rise and join him at the front. Her knees felt weak but she knew that she would be fine, if she could only make it to the front of the room and stand beside Menno.

The bishop cleared his throat and leveled his gaze at Menno as he began to enunciate the wedding vows. "Can you confess, brother, that you wish to take this our fellow-sister as your wedded wife, and not to part from her until death separates you, and that you believe this is from the Lord and that through your faith and prayers you have been able to come this far?"

Menno seemed to stiffen at the phrase *until death separate you* but he lifted his chin and loudly said, "Yes." His voice was strong and resonated throughout the room. There was no doubting his conviction in this decision.

The bishop turned his attention to Mary Ruth. "Can you confess, sister, that you wish to take this, our fellow-brother as your wedded husband, and not to part from him until death separates you, and that you believe this is from the Lord and that through your faith and prayers you have been able to come this far?"

She bit her lip and nodded her head. The word seemed stuck in her throat. But no one spoke until she finally forced out a soft "Yes" in response to the bishop's question.

"Since you, Menno Yoder, have confessed that you wish to take our fellow-sister to be your wedded wife, do you promise to be faithful to her and to care for her, even though she may suffer affliction, trouble, sickness, weakness, despair, as is so common among us poor humans, in a manner that befits a Christian and God-fearing husband?"

Menno did not hesitate to respond, "Yes."

Once again, the bishop turned back to Mary Ruth. "And you, Mary Ruth Fisher , you have also confessed that you wish to take our fellow-brother to be your wedded husband. Do you promise to be faithful to him and to care for him, even though he may suffer affliction, trouble, sickness, weakness, despair, as is so common among us poor humans, in a manner that befits a Christian and God-fearing wife?"

She glanced at Menno. He was staring straight ahead, the line of his jaw taunt as he waited for her response. "Yes," she said softly. She noticed that he relaxed ever so slightly.

The bishop took one step back and said, "Extend your right hand to each other." When they did so, he covered their hands with his and said, "The God of Abraham, the God of Isaac, and the God of Jacob be with you and help you come together and shed His blessing richly upon you. You may go forth as a married coupe. Fear God and keep His commandments."

And they were married.

Mary Ruth felt weak and tired. Her chest hurt and she realized that she had been holding her breath for what seemed like hours. Now, she could exhale properly and look at Menno, her husband. When she did, she saw a tear in his eye and a moment of panic rushed through her. *Was he regretting the decision already?*

He smiled at her and squeezed her hand. There was no marriage kiss or even an embrace, but despite the fact that the bishop was calling for a final prayer, Menno took a second to lean down, her hand still clenched in his, and, ever so softly, he whispered into her ear, "*Danke* Mary Ruth…my sweet wife."

Mimi had witnessed the gesture from Menno and something in her heart instantly warmed. Despite the whispers among the community, she sensed a deep emotional bond between Menno and his young bride. When Menno whispered into Mary Ruth's ear, Mimi had felt her own tears come to her eyes. She was pleased that Menno had found companionship again and prayed that it would turn into a love as deep as what she knew he had felt with Martha.

"Soon it will be your day," someone teased behind her back.

Mimi turned around and saw her friend Priscilla. "Oh ja, and you, too, no?"

Priscilla laughed. "Ja," she said, her eyes roaming the room for her future husband, Stephen Esh. They, too, had just been announced and their wedding was in December. Though older than Priscilla, Stephen Esh had not courted any other Amish woman. When Priscilla had turned sixteen, he was the first man to escort her from a singing and had made certain that his intentions were known to her from the beginning. It was as if he had been waiting for her all along.

Mimi sighed, watching Priscilla and Stephen's silent communication. "It's funny how things work, ain't so?" When Priscilla turned around to look at her, Mimi continued. "Last wedding season, I thought I'd never find the right man to marry. I didn't even know Steve Fisher then. Now, next week, I'm to become his wife."

Priscilla tilted her head and thought about that. "The Lord brought you together, that's for sure and certain."

"That He did," Mimi agreed.

She turned to look for Steve and saw that he was talking with her cousin Jonas. She watched him for a few minutes, trying to remember when she had first seen him at her daed's store. There had been something about him that had struck a chord with her, something that had made her decide to take a chance and call him to pick up the glass for his broken window. Her daed was usually the one that would make such a call. But not that time. In hindsight, it was truly the hand of God that had given her the strength to make that call. It was God who had guided Steve to not pursue other women. Instead, it was as if he had been waiting for the past ten or so years just for her. For a moment she felt truly overwhelmed.

She excused herself from Priscilla and started walking over to Steve. She needed to be near him, to talk to him. She was counting down the days until their wedding and was envious that, unlike Mary Ruth, she would not be able to live with him right away. Of course, most first marriages were that way. The bride lived with her parents until the house was ready to be occupied. Even Priscilla would not live with Stephen Esh until closer to spring when he had the farmhouse ready for occupancy.

Of course, on the weekends, the newly married couple would be together, again usually staying at the mother's house. Mimi knew that she would go to Steve's parents house, instead, since he needed to tend to their dairy barn over the weekend. She was looking forward to those mornings when she would wake up next to her new husband before the sun rose. Together, they would bundle up and head outside to walk down the lane and cross the street. In the darkness, they would light the lanterns in the barn and begin the tasks of feeding, watering, and milking his small herd of cows. That sounded right *gut* to her.

Later in the evenings, they would hitch the horse to the buggy and go visiting. Typically, young married couples might even stay overnight at their siblings, aunts, or uncles homes during those first weekends. Mimi was relieved that they wouldn't have to do that. There was a benefit to becoming the wife of an already established dairy farmer.

He smiled at her as she approached. "Did you have a chance to visit Mary Ruth and Menno, then?" he asked.

"Without you?" She laughed at him. "I wouldn't do such a thing, Steve Fisher !"

A sheepish look crossed his face. He had forgotten. As an engaged couple, they did certain things together as if they were already married, including approaching the corner table where Mary Ruth and Menno sat, accepting their meal from attendants and greeting the guests who went to visit them and offer their congratulations. Everyone had to visit the table in order to spend a moment with the newlyweds. In most cases, they went as a couple. Even unmarried Amish woman over the age of 16 would pair up with a young man to walk, hand in hand, to the table to express their warm wishes.

"We should go then, ja?" He touched her elbow and guided her through the people toward the back of the room where the Yoder's were seated.

Mary Ruth was picking at her food, simply pushing it around her plate. It was clear that she hadn't tasted anything on her plate. Not even the wedding cake that had been served to her.

She seemed quiet and uptight, timid and withdrawn. Her face was pale and her eyes large with worry. That was not the Mary Ruth that Steve had grown up with. Menno, however, was much more relaxed and greeted Steve and Mimi with a warm smile.

"Congratulations," Steve said as he reached to shake Menno's hand. He repeated the greeting to his sister.

"And to you," Menno said. His expression and demeanor reflected how he felt: comfortable and pleasant, the complete opposite of his new bride. "We will look forward to attending your wedding service next week."

Mary Ruth remained quiet but managed to force a smile at her brother and Mimi.

"I'm sure your sisters will come tomorrow to help ready up the place," Mimi said. "But I'd be happy to stop by to assist if you'd have a care."

Mary Ruth blinked as if not quite understanding what Mimi had said. Then in dawned on her. Typically, the bride was married at her parents' house. In the morning, the bride and groom helped the parents clean up from the wedding festivities. Since they had held the wedding service at Menno's home, there would be no one to help tidy up the dishes and reorganize the furniture.

"I...I hadn't thought about that," she said softly and glanced at Menno. "Leah has the *kinner*, she won't come help. And Rachel with Elijah..." Her voice trailed off and she waited for Menno to guide her.

He noticed her discomfort and, under the table, he reached for her hand. He was surprised that she clutched his hand, squeezing it tightly. One glance at her face told him all that he needed to know: Mary Ruth was a bundle of nerves. It dawned on him that he knew exactly why. This was a huge step for her and the realization had just hit her. When everyone left, she would stay behind for now she was his wife and the mamm to his children. She would have to take care of the house, the garden, the clothing, and the food...not just part-time, but for the rest of her life. She was scared and needed his support, needed his reassurance that she could do this and would not be compared to Martha.

Turning his attention back to Mimi, he nodded. "That would be right kind, Mimi. Maybe mid-morning if that suits?"

Menno knew that people wouldn't be leaving for another few hours. He wished that he could take Mary Ruth aside and talk to her, to reassure her and comfort her. However, that would not be proper to disappear from their wedding meal. So, as Steve and Mimi made their way back to their circle of friends, Menno leaned over, close to Mary Ruth's ear, and spoke in a low voice so that no one else could hear.

"Relax," he said. "It's all going to be fine."

She turned to look at him, his face just inches from hers. He was so much older than her and so confident. For days, even weeks, she had been feeling as if she could conquer this task but now, as the reality sunk in, she felt the butterflies in her stomach and pounding of her heart. "I..."

"Ssssh," he whispered. "Later. For now, enjoy your

wedding meal and the well-wishes of our friends and family." He gave her hand another squeeze and felt her fingers entwine with his. The gesture warmed his heart. She was trying. He could see that.

"Remember what you were saying the other day about love?" Melvin said, picking at his dessert plate.

Katie was seated next to him on the bench near the kitchen. The other children had finished already and were outside playing in the barn and yard. Despite the overcast skies, there wasn't a hint of rain in the air. "You mean with the pony, Butterscotch?"

He nodded, chewing the piece of pie he had just taken in his mouth. "Ja," he mumbled.

"What about it?" she asked, shrugging her shoulders.

"I don't think love is anything like how you feel about a pony," he said.

Katie frowned. "You don't?"

"*Nee*," he said firmly. "You feel that way about people, not ponies."

For a moment, Katie seemed to think about what Melvin had just said to her. She knew that she loved that pony. How could he deny that? But she also knew that, when she went to visit the pony, it was much more fun and special when Melvin went with her. In fact, when Melvin had left that day, Katie had lost interest in the pony. It was Melvin who made her heart jump and her smile brighten her face. It dawned on Katie that, perhaps, in a way, she loved Melvin.

"We're cousins now," Katie finally said. "But we were friends first."

"That's true, ja," he replied.

She frowned, still deep in thought. "One can certainly love

friends, ain't so? And one is definitely supposed to love family!"

Melvin smiled. He liked the direction that this conversation was headed. "I reckon you have a point, Katie."

She turned to look at him. "I'd say at our age it's right *gut* to have family-friends, wouldn't you say?"

He reached out and touched her hand, holding it lightly in his own. "You know what, cousin? I'd say you're right!"

They both laughed, each understanding what was being said without further words. He leaned over and knocked his shoulder against her and she returned the gesture. After the meal, they both knew that they would escape through the back pasture to the Miller's farm to take turns riding Butterscotch and this time, despite how she felt about the pony, Katie was well aware that it was because of Melvin that she kept coming back.

Miriam saw a huddle of her *dochders* near the back door, their heads bent together as they talked quietly amongst themselves. "Trouble," Miriam thought as she hurried over to them to find out what was brewing. When Lizzie, Leah and Rachel got together, it was important.

She was surprised to see Rachel crying. Rachel, the backbone of the family, so strong and unbending! She was a force to be taken seriously, the next matriarch of the entire family. Miriam always knew that the family could survive anything as long as Rachel was at the helm.

But now she was crying and that wasn't a good sign. "Rachel? What's wrong?"

She shook her head and, despite the tears, she laughed. "Nothing Mamm. Just the opposite!"

Miriam frowned. "You have some explaining to do then, *Dochder*, standing here crying at your sister's wedding meal."

"It's Elijah! He's decided to take the treatment." She covered her face with her hands, wiping the tears away as she laughed with relief. "He told me right after the service! Said he had to try to fight it. Couldn't imagine me marrying another man!" Again, the laughter.

Lizzie and Leah both consoled her, rubbing Rachel's arm and her back. Miriam understood what her *dochder* was feeling: relief that her husband was going to try to survive but fear that it wouldn't work.

"You need to pull it together," Miriam said softly. "People will wonder."

"Oh let them!" she said, laughing through her tears. "There is hope now. A chance. Even if it is small, I just needed that shred of hope."

"When will his treatment start?" Miriam asked.

There was no answer to that but Rachel knew that she would call straightaway in the morning, maybe even this very afternoon if she could excuse herself from the wedding festivities. "I'll let you know when the doctors can arrange it," she said. "I imagine it will be soon, ja?"

Collectively, they glanced at Elijah. He looked pale and weary as he rested in a chair that Menno had set out just for him. It was clear that he was struggling to stay awake. "You best be getting him home, Rachel. It sure was *gut* of him to make the effort, but now he needs his strength for a different fight," Miriam suggested. "And when you go with him for treatment, I'll come stay to tend the *kinner*. Can't have you worrying about two ends of the candle burning."

"Oh *danke*, Mamm," Rachel said, reaching out to embrace her mother, a rare display of affection. "I'm going to need you so if we are to get through this and survive," she whispered into her mamm's ear.

"If it's God's will," Miriam replied. "We will all survive."

It was late afternoon when everyone had started to leave. Even during wedding season, cows needed to be milked and all of the farm animals needed to be fed. After the last family had departed, Menno excused himself and went upstairs to change out of his Sunday suit. He, too, had chores that couldn't wait until the morning. With the sun setting earlier, there was no sense delaying and start chores in the dark.

Mary Ruth wasn't quite sure what to do. The benches had been put away, stored in the large grey wooden wagon in the backyard. But the rest of the furniture was still stored in the barn. The women had been kind enough to clean most of the dishes so that the kitchen was orderly. And the *kinner* had quietly disappeared, Melvin taking charge so that Menno and Mary Ruth had some time alone. She suspected that they had gone back to Leah's after visiting the Miller farm to see the pony.

Hesitating, she walked up the stairs, hating the way that they creaked. She could hear Menno moving about the bedroom. A dresser drawer opened. A shoe fell to the floor. The door was not shut all of the way and, her hand on the doorframe, she cleared her throat to make her presence known.

"Mary Ruth?"

She peeked around the corner then quickly looked away when she saw him sitting on the edge of the bed. "I...I didn't want to disturb you but I thought I'd see if you needed any help in the barn?"

He had been getting changed. His work shirt was unbuttoned at the throat and the suspenders from his black pants hung down by his sides. Standing up, he slid his arms into each strap and took a step toward her. In the small bedroom, he seemed taller, his presence filling the room.

Sensing her trepidation, Menno smiled gently and reached for her hand. He pulled her into the room and stood close to her, staring down into her face. He reached up and caressed her cheek with his thumb. "You were lovely today, Mary Ruth," he said, his blue eyes staring into hers. "And now you are my wife."

"Your wife," she repeated. The words sounded foreign and surreal. She barely knew this man and she had promised to be his wife for eternity, until death separated them. Yet, she knew so little about him. "Menno?" Her voice sounded small in the silence of the room.

"Yes?"

She turned her eyes away, staring at anything but him. She wanted one thing very much but she was afraid to ask. Still, she knew that she needed it in order to move past feeling so afraid and timid in his presence. The words, however, would not form on her lips.

He tilted her chin up so that she had to look at him. "What is it, Mary Ruth?"

"I…" She stumbled over the words, trying to gather the courage to ask. What would he think?

"Go on," he urged.

Taking a deep breath, she looked him square in the eye and found the strength to tell him what was on her mind. "I should like to know what it's like to kiss you." She paused. "To kiss my husband."

His lips twitched and she thought he was going to smile. Had her question amused him? After fighting so hard to tell him what she wanted, was he going to laugh? Yet, she knew it was better than if he thought she was too forward or brazen. That would not have gotten the marriage off on the right foot.

To her relief, he leaned down and gently brushed his lips

against hers. The kiss was light and soft, tender and sweet, his whiskers tickling her chin. There was no urgency or compromise in the kiss. It spoke of new beginnings with no hurry to end. Then, he pulled her into his arms and hugged her, her body pressed against his. For a long moment, he held her like that and she felt herself relax. She felt safe and warm in his arms. He would protect her and take care of her.

When he stepped backward, he looked down at her and she was surprised to see tears in his eyes. At first, she wondered if they were of sorrow or regret. She reached her hand out to wipe one away but he grabbed her hand and pressed his lips against her palm.

"Don't," he whispered, his voice hoarse. "Those are happy tears. Happy tears for God bringing you into our lives. I don't claim to understand His ways or why He took Martha when He did. But you have truly saved us and I know that God has His reasons." He leaned down one more time to kiss her, this time on the forehead before he held her facing him and, looking deep into her eyes he heard himself say: "*Danke*, Mary Ruth. And *danke* God."

Abruptly, he released her and took a step backward as if trying to compose himself. He seemed embarrassed by his own emotion and Mary Ruth found herself fascinated. There were so many sides to this man, so much to learn.

"Now," he said, clearing his throat. "You asked if you could help in the barn. That's awful kind of you, Mary Ruth, but I won't have my *fraa* helping with chores on her wedding day. You spend your time unpacking your things," he said, gesturing toward the corner where two small bags were waiting. "I'll bring your hope chest in from the back room tomorrow. I'll be anxious to see what you have inside," he asked. "And if you need anything else to make the house feel like home, we can discuss it and plan accordingly, ja?"

He started to walk out of the room but Mary Ruth called out, "Menno?"

He stopped and turned back. "Ja?"

"I...I love you," she said shyly.

Her words caught him off guard and he seemed to think about them for a moment. Then, with a hint of a smile and a wink, he replied, "Mayhaps. But if not, you will." And he was gone, his heavy shoes thumping on the stairs, each one creaking under his weight, as he hurried down to the kitchen for a glass of water before heading outside to the barn.

She stood at the bedroom window, watching her new husband as he crossed the barnyard. From inside the barn, the *kinner* saw him and ran to greet him, young Emma tripping over her own feet. Menno paused and helped her up, brushing the dust from her dress before giving her a hug. He pointed to the house and said something before Emma ran toward it. He glanced up and saw Mary Ruth at the window, her eyes taking in the scene.

A warm smile flashed across his face and he lifted his hand to her. She pressed her own hand against the window, just as she heard the kitchen door open and a small voice call out, "Mamm! I need a Band-Aid please!"

Miriam sat at her kitchen table, the package of letters scattered over the table. Her fingers touched each one and her eyes skimmed over them.

Each letter, written by a different family, was written in different penmanship about their very different lives. When Miriam had started the circle letters, she had no idea how far the family would come in such a short period of time. Mary Ruth was married and wouldn't be returning. Steve was to marry next week and, although he would not be leaving for his own farm right away,

Mimi would be coming to visit on the weekends and, Miriam suspected, would most likely stay before long. John David and Ella were waiting to married in December and would move into their new farm in the spring.

Life would settle down on the Fisher farm for a while until new babies were born and older children began their *rumschpringe*. Before long, the next cycle of marriages would begin.

For the first time in a very long time, Miriam felt tired. It was not the kind of *tired* one would inevitably experience after a long day of household chores, or working in the fields only to come home and tend to the dairy barn. No, it definitely wasn't that. It was more like a mental fatigue; the outcome of an inner struggle filled with dilemmas, difficult decisions to ponder and unavoidable acceptance of what could not be undone. But perhaps the "undoing" was not quite hers to judge or to decide, after all?

Indeed, together with Elias, she had been at the helm of their family for so long, now. A pillar of moral support. She had been a good wife to Elias and a good mother to their children. A matriarch of sorts. Yet, together with that mental fatigue came a peaceful sensation; a sensation of having rightly stood by her beliefs, of having done her very best to raise her children right gut, the way she herself had been raised and her parents before her, true to her faith in the Creator, true to her Amish heritage.

And, looking at all those letters with these very different yet so familiar handwritings, some of which that she had herself helped forge and strengthen throughout the years, Miriam Fisher came to realize that this circle that she had started just a few months ago, this *circle of letters* was, actually, her own *circle of life.*

The Sequel

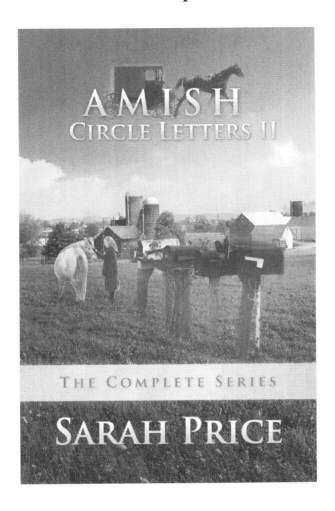

Click here to order
Amish Circle Letters II: The Second Circle of Letters.

Recipes

Amish Meadow Tea

Recipe from Miriam Fisher

1. Boil one gallon of water.
2. When bubbling, put in a healthy handful of mint tea leaves from garden (about two huge fistful of cuttings).
3. Take off of the heat and let sit for 7 minutes.
4. Remove tea leaves from water.
5. Add 1.5 cups of sugar (more or less to suit your taste).
6. Put pot of water in a sink of cooler water (to cool down).
7. Refrigerate before serving.
8. Might need to be adjusted to accommodate your needs.

HINT: Growing tea plants in your garden is a wonderful adventure but be careful. Tea can take over your garden. You also need to cut the stalks BEFORE they flower. If they get spindly looking, cut them down and they will grow back. Most tea gardens can get 2-3 batches each season.

Amish Corn Flake Sugar Cookies

Recipe from Rachel Fisher Zook

Ingredients

- 1 cup shortening
- 1 ¾ cups brown sugar
- 2 eggs
- 2 cups flour
- ½ teaspoon salt
- 3 teaspoons baking powder
- ½ cup whole milk
- 2 cups corn flakes
- 1 teaspoon vanilla

Directions

1. Preheat oven to 375 degrees.
2. After creaming the shortening and sugar together, add the eggs and vanilla. Beat until mixture is light and fluffy.
3. In a separate bowl, mix together all of the dry ingredients (except corn flakes). Sifting is recommended.
4. Add corn flakes to the dry ingredients and mix by hand.
5. Add dry ingredients and milk to the cream mixture. Stir until smooth.
6. Use a soupspoon or melon ball maker to drop the mixture onto a greased baking sheet. Leave space between each, as they will spread when cooking.
7. Bake for 10-12 minutes and let cool before serving.

Shoofly Pie

Recipe from Leah Fisher Miller

Ingredients

- 2 cups molasses
- 2 cups hot water
- 3 cup light brown sugar
- 1.5 teaspoon soda
- 5 cups flour
- 1 cup shortening
- .5 teaspoon cream of tartar
- 3-4 unbaked pie shells

Directions

1. Preheat oven to 450 degrees.

2. Mix molasses, hot water, 1 cup light brown syrup, and 1 teaspoon soda together. This is the syrup for the bottom of the pie.

3. Mix the rest of the ingredients. This is the crumb topping.

4. Pour the syrup into unbaked pie shells.

5. Divide crumbs on top.

6. Bake for 10 minutes then lower heat to 350 and bake for an hour.

Apple Crunch[5]

Recipe from Anna Fisher

Ingredients

- 5 to 6 apples, pared and sliced
- 1 cup flour
- 1 1/2 cups sugar
- 1 tsp baking powder
- 3/4 tsp salt
- 1 egg
- 1/3 cup butter or margarine, melted and cooled
- 1 tsp cinnamon

Directions

1. Place apples in a 9X13 inch baking dish.
2. Mix next 5 ingredients with a fork until crumbly.
3. Sprinkle over apples.
4. Pour melted butter or margarine over mixture.
5. Sprinkle with cinnamon.
6. Bake at 350 degrees for 30 to 40 minutes.

---

[5] Submitted by PJ Rodgers.

Cinnamon Minis[6]

Recipe from Lizzie Fisher Stoltzfus

Ingredients

- 2 cups flour
- 2/3 cup & 2 tbsp. Crisco
- 6 tbsp. water
- 1 stick butter- softened
- 1 cup sugar
- 1-2 tbsp. cinnamon

Directions

1. In a large bowl, add flour and cut in Crisco. When flour and Crisco are combined well, add in water and form into dough ball. Lightly flour the working surface.
2. Roll dough into a ¼" thick rectangle shape.
3. Spread butter over entire surface (more butter can be added if desired).
4. Mix together sugar and cinnamon. Coat the entire rectangle with the sugar mixture.
5. Tightly roll your dough and then cut into slices about a half-inch thick.
6. Bake at 350 degrees for 30 minutes or until golden brown.

---

[6] Submitted by Kris Behringer.

Lima Bean and Corn Salad

Recipe from Sylvia Fisher Esh

Ingredients

- 1 cup butter, divided
- 2 cups fresh (or previously frozen) lima beans
- ½ teaspoon salt
- ¼ teaspoon pepper
- 4 fresh tomatoes, peeled and chopped
- 2 teaspoons white sugar
- 2 cups fresh (or previously frozen) corn kernels, cut from the cob

Directions

Melt 1/2 cup butter in a large saucepan over medium heat. Stir in lima beans, salt, and pepper. Cook for approximately 20 minutes, testing the lima beans to make certain they are tender. In a separate saucepan, heat tomatoes, sugar and remaining 1/2 cup butter. Cook until tomatoes are tender (approximately 15-20 minutes). Combine the tomatoes into lima beans and add corn. Cook 10 minutes more. Serve hot or at room temperature.

Pennsylvania Dutch Potato Filling[7]

Recipe from Lovina Fisher Weaver

Ingredients

- 6-8 med. Potatoes
- 1 med/large onion
- 1 stick butter for sauté and 1/2 stick for pats on top before putting in oven
- 1 c. milk
- 2 slices white bread, torn in sm. pieces and soak in 2/3 cup milk
- 1 lg. egg
- 1 bunch curly parsley
- Salt & pepper

Directions

1. Boil potatoes in salted water until done. Sauté chopped onion and cut up parsley in butter until soft and yellow.

2. Drain potatoes and mash using about 1/3 cup milk. Mix in sautéed onion parsley and butter, bread, egg and parsley.

3. Season to taste with salt and pepper. Thin to desired consistency with the rest of the milk. Beat thoroughly for a minute or two.

4. Pile in buttered baking dish. Dot with butter. Bake in 350 degree oven for approximately 1 hour.

5. Serve with gravy and any kind of meat and vegetables. Serves 8, to make enough for more, double the recipe.

---

[7] Submitted by Jane Knepp Dysput

Amish Chow-Chow

Recipe from Ella Riehl

Ingredients:

- 1 cup of the following: lima beans, cauliflower, onions cucumber, green beans, yellow beans, and carrots
- 1/4 c. salt
- 2 tsp. mustard seed
- 2 tsp. celery seed
- 2 c. vinegar
- 2 c. sugar

Directions

1. Cook all of the vegetable ingredients until tender.
2. Drain and let cool.
3. Chop them until they are same size.
4. Mix all ingredients.
5. Heat to a boil.
6. Best served cold.
7. To store, pack in jars and seal by boiling jars in water for at least ten minutes.

Amish Apple Crisp
Recipe from Mimi Hostetler

Ingredients:
- 6 large apples
- ¾ cup sugar
- ¾ tsp. salt
- 1 tsp. baking powder
- 1 large egg
- 1/3 cup cream
- Dash of cinnamon

Directions

1. Preheat oven to 350 degrees.
2. Peel, core, and slice the apples.
3. Arrange in a 9x13-baking pan.
4. Mix together the sugar, salt, baking powder and egg. Combine with the apples.
5. Pour the cream on top and sprinkle with cinnamon.
6. Bake for 30 minutes or until apples are done.

Amish Wedding Cake

Ingredients:

- 1 cup sugar
- 1 1/2 cups flour
- 1/2 cup milk
- 1/2 teaspoon salt
- 1 cup dates (pitted)
- 1/2 cup chopped walnuts
- 1 teaspoon vanilla extract
- 1 1/2 teaspoons baking powder
- 2 cups brown sugar
- 2 cups water
- 5 tablespoons butter

Directions

1. Preheat oven to 375 degrees.
2. Grease a 9x13 baking pan.
3. Combine the sugar, flour, milk, salt, dates, nut, vanilla and baking powder. Mix well to avoid lumps.
4. Pour the batter into the prepared pan.
5. In a saucepan, combine the brown sugar, water and butter. Bring to boil.
6. Pour brown sugar mixture (step 5) over batter.
7. Bake for 30 minutes or until apples are done. and serve with whipped cream.

One More Thing...

If you enjoyed this book, I'd be very grateful if you'd post a short review on Amazon. Your support really does make a difference. Not only do I read all the reviews in order to see what you liked and how I can improve, but they are also a great source of motivation. When I hear from my readers and fans, it really makes me want to keep writing...just for you.

If you'd like to leave a review or see a list of my books on Amazon, simply click here. And don't forget to follow me on Facebook so that you can hear firsthand about new, upcoming releases.

With blessings,

Sarah Price

http://www.facebook.com/fansofsarahprice

Hymn from the Ausbund

O God Father, we praise You
And Your goodness exalt,
With You, O Lord, so graciously
Have manifested to us anew,
And have brought us together, Lord,
To admonish us through Your Word,
Grant us grace to this.

Open the mouth, Lord, of Your servants,
Moreover grant them wisdom
That they may rightly speak Your Word,
Which ministers to a godly life
And is useful to Your glory,
Give us hunger for such nourishment,
That is our desire.

Give our hearts understanding as well,
Enlightenment here on earth,
That your Word be ingrained in us,
That we may become godly
And live in righteousness,
Heeding Your Word at all times,
So we will remain undeceived.

Yours, O Lord, is the kingdom alone,
And the power altogether.
We praise You in the assembly,

Giving thanks to your name,

And beseech You from the depths of our hearts

That You would be with us at this hour

Through Jesus Christ, Amen[8]

---

[8] Ausbund, Song 131. Also known as the *Lob Lieb,* this hymn is sung at every church service. In an Amish church service, it is sung in High German.

Glossary of Pennsylvania Dutch

Ach vell	An expression similar to *Oh Well*
Aendi	Aunt
Ausbund	Amish hymnal
Boppli	Baby
Bruder	Brother
Daed	Father
Danke	Thank you
Englische	Non-Amish people
Englischer	A non-Amish person
Ferhoodled	Confused
Fraa	Wife
G'may	Church district
Grossdaadi	Grandfather
Grossdaadihaus	Small house attached to the main house
Grossmammi	Grandmother
Gut	Good
Gut mariye	Good morning
Gut nochmidawk	Good afternoon
Ja	Yes
Kinner	Children
Leddich	Unmarried man
Lob Lieb	A special hymn sung during church
Mamm	Mother
Nee	No
Onkel	Uncle
Ordnung	Unwritten rules that govern the g'may
Rumschpringe	Period of "fun" time for youths
Schwester	Sister
Wie gehts?	What's going on?

Excerpt from Plain Fame

Sarah Price's Best-Selling Book

An Amazon Top 100 Book
(Book One of the Plain Fame Trilogy)
Available on amazon.com, BN.com, and kobo.com

Chapter One

New York City was as crowded as ever and traffic was backed-up for miles. Alejandro leaned his head back onto the plush headrest of his private limousine and shut his eyes for a few moments. After weeks of traveling, he was tired. Tired of living out of quickly packed suitcases, tired of hotels, tired of the lack of privacy. He missed the heart-warming sun, the long sandy beaches and the quiet of his own home in beautiful Miami. He made a mental note to remind his assistant to stop scheduling these trips for a while. He just needed some time to recuperate, to take a step back, to re-examine his life and to recharge his batteries.

"*Ay mi madre,*" he said to himself. Then, leaning forward, he tapped on the glass that separated him from his driver. "*¿Qué está pasando? ¿Por qué hay tanto tráfico?*" He couldn't imagine why there was so much traffic at this hour. It wasn't even noon and well past morning rush hour. Yet, the streets were packed, bumper-to-bumper. Even more frustrating were the pedestrians, ignoring traffic signals and crossing when they shouldn't. That was adding to the traffic. Alejandro sighed. He was going to be late.

The driver glanced back and shrugged his shoulders in the casual manner of a typical New Yorker. "Traffic, my man. It's just traffic."

"Dios mio," Alejandro complained under his breath. "We are going to make it in time, si?" His voice was deep and husky but thick with a Spanish accent. To the knowing linguist, he was Cuban. To the average American, he was just another Hispanic.

"Yeah, yeah, don't sweat it," the driver said.

Don't sweat it, Alejandro repeated to himself and shook his head. Spoken by a man who drives a limousine for a living, he thought. "If I'm late..." he said but chose not to complete the sentence. In reality, so what if he was late? It was only a meeting with Richard Gray, the largest music producer in America. But it was Richard Gray who had contacted him, Alejandro Diaz. It was Richard Gray who had requested the meeting, a lunch meeting, and that took all of the pressure off of Alejandro's shoulders. He was in control of this one. He was being sought after by the big man.

The stretch limousine lurched forward and the driver started to finally regain some speed. The traffic seemed to be breaking up somewhat, permitting the driver to make up some time and Alejandro began to relax. They'd get there on time. It was only twenty blocks from the hotel to the restaurant where the meeting was to take place. But they still had to pass through Times Square and 7th Avenue by Madison Square Garden.

"Don't these people work?" Alejandro grumbled as he began fiddling with his cell phone. Three texts from his manager and two from his agent. He was lucky. It was usually triple that amount. A slow day. *Must be a Tuesday*, he thought grimly. The only slow day of the week. And still, he had meetings and appointments and emails and text messages. When had life started to get so crazy, he asked himself.

He heard the crash before he actually recognized the jolt for what it was. The driver had slammed on his brakes, the car screeching to a halt, but not before the thud on the hood of the car made it apparent that something had been hit. Alejandro fell forward, despite the fact that the limo had not been driving over twenty miles an hour, if that. When he picked himself up from the floor and sat back on the black leather seat, he tried to assess what had happened.

"You all right back there?" the driver asked, his voice shaking and his face pale.

"*Sí, sí,*" Alejandro said, trying to calm himself. An accident. What were the odds of that? And why today of all days? He glanced around but didn't see another vehicle in front of the limousine. "What happened?"

"Hit someone. A jaywalker," the driver replied before picking up his cell phone and dialing 9-1-1.

The crowd was already gathering around the front of the car. People. There were always crowds of people around when he wanted them, but especially when he didn't. This was one of those moments. Alejandro exhaled loudly. Now he'd definitely be late. There was no way that he could get out of the limousine in this crowd without being recognized and that would be the kiss of death. He could see the headlines already: *Viper Strikes Pedestrian in Manhattan.*

He tried to do a quick calculation of how the next hour or two would pan out. The police would come and want to interview him. The crowd would gather, the traffic would be thick, and it would become a mob scene. He'd have no choice but to get out. Alejandro sighed, reaching into his suit pocket for his black sunglasses. If he had to get out and face the crowd, better to do it early on rather than look like he was avoiding it. And when the inevitable lawsuit happened, it would look better if he had seemed concerned. With that, the decision was made.

"What are you doing, sir?" The driver had turned around, just about to say something when he noticed Alejandro reaching for the door handle. There was panic in his voice. "You can't get out, sir. They'll notice you. There will be a mob!"

Alejandro nodded. "Exactly. But if I delay, that will be

even worse than if I get out now." It would be a different headline then: *Viper Indifferent to Struck Pedestrian in Manhattan.* That would never do; so, ignoring the concern of his driver, he pulled at the door handle and flung the door back, careful to not hit anyone who was standing nearby.

It took a second, maybe two, for the beginning of the murmuring to trickle through the crowd. He heard it, the gentle hum of recognition. Whispers, looks, people pointing, and then the name: Viper. They were already talking about him. Alejandro ignored it and hurried to the front of the car. He pushed past several people, making certain to say "Excuse me" as he did so. Manners, his mother had always taught him. No matter what the situation, a man had to be civilized and mannerly. When he finally got to the front of the limousine, he noticed two men leaning over a woman.

"Is she all right?" he asked, pulling at his pants as he knelt down beside them.

"She's hurt bad," one man said, glancing over his shoulder at Alejandro. He frowned as if recognizing him but turned his attention back to the woman.

"But is she responding?" Alejandro asked. He reached out for the woman's hand. Holding it in his, he was glad to feel her fingers twitch and clutch at his hand. He looked at her quickly. Her face was rolled to the side and her eyes were closed. The color had drained from her cheeks and her brown hair, pulled back from her face, gave a sharp contrast to her pale skin. There was no blood and for that, he gave a quick prayer of gratitude to God, but she was laying in a crumpled heap, one of her legs twisted in a crooked fashion from beneath her pale blue dress over which she wore a black apron. "My driver called for an ambulance. I wouldn't recommend moving her until they get here."

The driver was standing on the other side of the woman. "They said five minutes." He looked around at the traffic. It was even worse now since the limousine was blocking the intersection. "Like to see how they'll manage that."

As Alejandro continued to hold the woman's hand, he became well aware that people were beginning to take photographs. He frowned and motioned toward the driver. "Give me your jacket."

"What?"

"Your jacket! To cover her. They're starting to take photos," Alejandro snapped, trying to keep his voice down so that he was not overheard.

The driver quickly shook his black jacket off of his shoulders and handed it to Alejandro. Carefully, he laid it over the woman, hiding her face from the people who were taking pictures with their cell phones.

"Is she dressed in a costume?" the driver asked.

Alejandro looked up, caught off-guard by the question. "Costume?"

"She looks like Dorothy from the Wizard of Oz."

"She's Amish, you idiot," someone said from the crowd that was now forming on the sidewalk.

Alejandro wanted to ask what "Amish" was but didn't want to draw further attention to himself or to the situation than what was needed. Right now, all the media could say was that his driver hit the woman and he, Alejandro Diaz, had stayed by her side until the ambulance came. The police would soon arrive, question him, and then he'd be on his merry way to his meeting with Richard Gray. The worse thing that could happen is some minor damage to his bad-boy image.

The woman fluttered her eyes, trying to make sense of what was happening as she began to awaken. The color started to come back to her cheeks. Her chocolate brown eyes tried to make sense of all the people staring at her from above. "Where am I?" she asked.

"Oz, according to that guy!" someone from the crowd quipped.

Alejandro glared over his shoulder at the man who was laughing then looked back at the woman from behind his dark sunglasses. "You've been hit by a car," he said gently. "Don't try to move. Help is on the way, *princesa*."

But she didn't listen. When she tried to lift her head, she winced and fell back down to the street. "My leg," she whimpered, collapsing against Alejandro's body. He was still holding her hand and she clung to it, her head buried against his leg.

Alejandro lowered his voice. "You're going to be fine, but wait for the medical people. You can't move, *princesa*." He stared at her face, tanned with some freckles over the tops of her cheeks. She was fresh looking, like a country girl. The driver was right. She did resemble Dorothy with her blue dress and black apron. Except she had a white heart-shaped covering for her head that had been knocked off and laid in the middle of the street, a tourist stepping on one of the strings.

When she looked at him again, her dark eyes trying to make sense of what was happening to her, he felt a jolt. For as young and fresh as she was, she was also remarkably beautiful in a natural way that completely took him by surprise. Her tan skin glowed in the sun-rays that trickled through the skyscrapers. Her dark hair was pulled back from her face, a few loose strands curling down her neck. No make-up or fancy hair styles. Just a plain beauty that caught him off guard.

"My family," she whispered, moisture at the corner of her eyes.

"May I call someone for you?" His voice was soft, almost a whisper so that the people surrounding them couldn't hear, as he tightened his grasp on her hand. He was surprised when she clasped it, her grip strong, and he found himself staring into her face, once again amazed at how beautiful she looked.

Despite the clear pain that she was in, the young woman was still stoic and dignified, hiding her discomfort. Yet, when she tried to shake her head, a single tear trickled down her cheek. "We don't have a phone. They need to know," she said, her voice trailing off.

No phone? Not even a cell phone? He frowned but didn't inquire further. He could hear the sirens in the distance. He imagined the police would arrive first and, from that point on, he'd be questioned then able to leave. Another thirty minutes, he thought. Forty-five, tops.

"What is your name, *princesa*?"

"Amanda," she whispered. "Amanda Beiler."

Alejandro nodded, aware that she had a slight accent. He couldn't quite place it. It wasn't European and certainly it wasn't from South America. But it was different from the other American accents. "If you tell me your address, I'll make certain that a message gets to your family."

She clutched his hand and he leaned forward. "Creek Road in Lititz, Pennsylvania." She paused, shutting her eyes as tears started to well at the corners. "They think I'll be home tonight for my chores."

He laughed softly and caressed her hand with his thumb. "You won't be home for chores tonight, Amanda Beiler. But you'll be just fine." He paused before adding, "I'll make sure of it." She was the image of innocence and clearly a long way from home. While he knew nothing about Lititz, Pennsylvania, he suspected it was far from Philadelphia or Pittsburgh. And certainly not close to New York City. "I promise," he heard himself say.

He could hear the mumbling behind him. The crowd was beginning to liven up. If people hadn't recognized him before, he knew the word was now floating through the crowd. He could sense the energy as more people began to peer over the heads of others, trying to see him, trying to take a photograph of him. The cell phones were in the air snapping photos of Alejandro kneeling beside the Amish woman on the streets of Manhattan. *No,* he corrected himself. *Photos of Viper with the Amish woman.* Alejandro wondered which one would wind up on the entertainment channels and the tabloids later on this evening.

The police arrived moments later, their cars making their way through the crowded streets, avoiding the pedestrians who didn't seem to care that they were breaking the law by darting across the road. Once the police had parked their cars, ignoring the other drivers who began honking their horns at being blocked and delayed, two policemen began to push the crowd back, creating a buffer so that the ambulance would be able to get through when it arrived. Another police officer approached Alejandro, quickly assessing that he was a good person to start interviewing.

"What happened here, sir?"

Alejandro glanced up, peering at the officer from behind his dark sunglasses. He tried to pick his words carefully, knowing that too many people were probably recording the scene. What he said now would most likely be replayed over and over again, on television, on interviews, and in court when the young woman sued for having been hit by his driver.

"I'm not exactly certain," Alejandro said. "I just know that she was hit by the limousine."

The officer peered at him for a moment. It was the moment of recognition. "Aren't you..?"

And so it begins, he thought wistfully. Avoiding the question, Alejandro glanced at the woman. "No disrespect," he said. "But she's in a lot of pain, Officer. Do you have any idea when the ambulance will get here?"

To Alejandro's relief, the officer leaned his chin over to his shoulder, talking into his walkie-talkie. While the officer was trying to get a reading on the location of the ambulance, Alejandro turned his attention back to the young woman. "Amanda?" he asked softly. "Amanda? You hanging in there, *princesa*?"

She nodded slightly. Her face was pale and tears now fell freely down her cheeks. "I just wanted a pair of sunglasses," she said, her words barely audible.

"What?" He leaned down, trying to hear what she was saying. "What did you say?"

She reached for his hand again, holding it tightly in her own. "While I was waiting for my train," she whispered. "I was crossing the street for a pair of sunglasses."

He didn't have an opportunity to ask her about what she had said. The ambulance was pulling up behind them, the horn beeping for people to get out of the way. The officer in charge motioned for Alejandro to back away so that the paramedics could bring the gurney closer.

Respectfully, he moved back but stopped just a few feet from where she was stretched out on the road. He noticed the white cap laying on the ground a few feet away and stooped to pick it up. Clutching it into his hands, Alejandro watched as the paramedics worked, quickly taking her vital signs and asking a rapid barrage of questions. Within minutes, Amanda Beiler was gently lifted from the streets of Manhattan, placed on the crisp white sheet covering the gurney, and whisked away to a hospital.

Alejandro stared after it, too aware that his cell phone was vibrating in his pocket and the officer was asking him a question. But his mind was elsewhere. This young woman, dressed in such plain clothes and with such a pure, fresh look on her face, lingered in his memory and he found that he could think of nothing else. She was alone in Manhattan and clearly out of her element. He knew the feeling from his own days as an immigrant with his mother in Miami. And he also knew that he wasn't going to make that appointment with Richard Gray. Only this was now by his own choice, not because of being delayed by the accident.

About Sarah Price

The Preiss family emigrated from Europe in 1705, settling in Pennsylvania as the area's first wave of Mennonite families. Sarah Price has always respected and honored her ancestors through exploration and research about her family's history and their religion. At nineteen, she befriended an Amish family and lived on their farm throughout the years.

Twenty-five years later, Sarah Price splits her time between her home outside of New York City and an Amish farm in Lancaster County, PA where she retreats to reflect, write, and reconnect with her Amish friends and Mennonite family.

Find Sarah Price on Facebook and Goodreads!
Learn about upcoming books, sequels, series, and contests!

Contact the author at sarahprice.author@gmail.com.
Visit her weblog at http://www.sarahpriceauthor.com or
on Facebook at www.facebook.com/fansofsarahprice.

MIRRIAM

Jacob + Amna (Katie)

Steve Fisher (35) - sweet on Mimi
                    (Farm Store)

Rachael (oldest) - lives near Leah (sista)
         down road from mimms + older

Mimms - Melvin -
        - martha died had baker

Mary Ruth (younger daughter) helping
   sister Leah — taking care of young kids

Leah - lazy sister - has 6 kids - one
         (Jonah (husband)   down

Lizzie outspoken - next to Rachael
   in age.

Silvia - one of the brothers wives

Levina + James (older bro) — No
   younger   Kids

Elena Hale - English woman c̄
   horses - has - pony Katie will
   look after

Benjamin - Elder in Church

Friends

Made in the USA
San Bernardino, CA
02 August 2014